The RIGHT LENS

Satyajit Senapati is a best-selling author, TEDx speaker, and seasoned corporate leader with over two decades of experience across top management consulting firms and global conglomerates. An MBA from IIM Lucknow, he has led high-impact teams, driven strategic transformations, and shaped leadership narratives in some of the world's most respected organizations.

Satyajit's writing draws from his deep corporate experience and his passion for making complex ideas simple and actionable. His books—*Work, Workmanship & Winning* and *The Leader's Kaleidoscope*—have helped thousands of professionals navigate the evolving world of work and leadership.

Off the page, he is a sought-after keynote speaker and an active voice on social media, where his insights on careers, leadership, and personal growth have garnered over 10 million views. With a calm voice and a curious mind, Satyajit invites readers to reflect, rethink, and redesign the way they approach life and work.

The RIGHT LENS

Life Themes to Pause,
Reflect and Begin Again

SATYAJIT SENAPATI

Published by
Rupa Publications India Pvt. Ltd 2025
7/16, Ansari Road, Daryaganj
New Delhi 110002

Sales centres:
Bengaluru Chennai
Hyderabad Jaipur Kathmandu
Kolkata Mumbai Prayagraj

Copyright © Satyajit Senapati 2025

The views and opinions expressed in this book are the author's own and the facts are as reported by him; these have been verified to the extent possible, and the publishers are not in any way liable for the same.

All rights reserved.

No part of this publication may be reproduced, transmitted, or stored in a retrieval system, in any form or by any means, electronic, mechanical, photocopying, recording or otherwise, without the prior permission of the publisher.

P-ISBN: 978-93-7003-242-2
E-ISBN: 978-93-7003-146-3

First impression 2025

10 9 8 7 6 5 4 3 2 1

The moral right of the author has been asserted.

Printed in India

This book is sold subject to the condition that it shall not, by way of trade or otherwise, be lent, resold, hired out, or otherwise circulated, without the publisher's prior consent, in any form of binding or cover other than that in which it is published.

*To Baba and Maa for being a constant source of guidance.
To Smaranika, Sanskriti and Sonali for being
there through thick and thin.*

Contents

Glass Half-Full? An Introduction / ix

1. Success / 1

2. Setbacks / 25

3. Identity: Who Am I? / 48

4. Decisions / 64

5. Hobbies and Interests / 79

6. Seeking Help / 92

7. Giving Back to Society / 103

8. Relationship with Career / 112

9. Freedom / 131

10. The Right Lens / 141

Acknowledgements / 145

Glass Half-Full?

An Introduction

I think we can all agree that life throws us curveballs every now and then. Each time you will need a special effort and a different perspective to get out of the abyss. This is what is called personal transformation, which you are likely to experience many times in your life. Yes, you heard it right—many times.

What happens when you go through a personal transformation? Is it a one-off phenomenon? What can help you on this very personal journey? How do you undertake this transformation? What is the outcome?

These are some key questions that I have humbly attempted to address in this book.

To put forward my reasons for writing this book, I need to take you back in time and start with the narrative from my student days. Don't worry, it may sound like 100 years, but trust me, it is not.

I was a good student. You know the ones who are the good boys in the class. The ones who study hard, get good grades, and do not pick up fights. I was one of them. I studied hard, did well in school, got into a good college, and did well there too. When placement time came, I prepared hard and got into a company of my choice where my skills were aligned to the job.

Life was suddenly exciting. Fresh at workplace, nothing to worry about, and my own money to spend—it was all so much fun. I worked hard for a few years, and then the itch to do an MBA led me to a B-school where I completed my MBA and joined a top management consulting firm. Thereafter, one role led to another, one country to another, and one company to another. My professional career was going great. Apart from those usual moments of 'Who am I? What am I doing? What is my purpose?', my professional life was on track with the usuals—hikes and promotions—all of it coming at the right time.

Then an opportunity in the form of a global leadership role in a multinational corporation came, and I felt blessed to have been given this chance in my career. Global role, great compensation, excellent MNC culture—what else could I ask for? I felt like I had arrived.

I started the new assignment with a lot of enthusiasm and energy amid COVID-19 lockdown and restrictions. After some time, I decided to visit my hometown, as I had not been there for more than a year because of the pandemic. I planned the visit in March 2021, just as the second wave gripped the world.

It is always a great feeling to meet parents, especially after a long time. Little did I know what was waiting for me around the corner.

In 2021, my mother fell victim to COVID. She was getting

treatment at home, and one morning her blood oxygen level dropped so low that we had to move her to the intensive care unit. She was getting better. The doctor assured us she would be moved from the ICU back to the room. We were looking forward to her return. Instead, the following afternoon, the doctor called and informed us that she was no more and had died of a cardiac arrest.

We were shocked.

The news of my mother's death came unexpectedly, and the entire family was in utter disbelief. What followed was an extremely difficult time for us.

After a couple of days, my father, my wife, my daughter and I contracted COVID. For me and my wife, the case was a little complicated as we also developed chest infection.

Although all of us sprung back to health in a month's time and were fortunate to survive the deadly virus, for me it was just the beginning. After I was cured of COVID, I got a fungal infection, followed by a bacterial and a viral infection, and this cycle continued for months. It was so intense and draining that at one time I felt that I would never get back to my healthy self again.

Around this time, things on the job front were not going too well either. I had two ways to move forward at my job— find a new project or find a new job. Unfortunately, I was not in a position to pursue either, and hence I bid goodbye to the job, which I had worked so hard to get.

In life, one setback is good enough to derail us from track, and it takes a lot to get back on it. Here I was facing three major setbacks simultaneously—the loss of a loved one, battling complicated health issues, and dealing with the absence of engagement that comes with a job. I had been working for eighteen years.

Honestly speaking, I did not know where I was or what I would do next; it was like being in the 'dark trenches' without knowing if there was a streak of light at the end of it.

The triple setbacks took a toll on me. Day by day, the darkness of the trenches got darker.

When you go through a difficult time, it drains you both mentally and physically. You tend to ask for help and expect a magic hand to get you out of the situation, but unfortunately that does not happen. Slowly, day by day, your optimism dies, and you spiral into a vicious circle of self-doubt, hopelessness and despondency. Perhaps it is the universe's way of telling you that you must travel this journey alone.

For some, the realization comes like a thunderclap—a quick, sharp jolt—and they find themselves saying, 'I have had enough.' For others, it could be a slow and arduous process, much like painting where each brushstroke gradually shapes a new perspective. The exact point of the realization may not be highly pronounced, but may get triggered by a simple moment, such as a heartfelt conversation, a motivating line from a book, a song lyric that unexpectedly resonates, or even sheer exhaustion from the constant weight of despair.

In my case, the realization was a mix of both. The triple setbacks made me feel like a victim of fate. I found myself constantly thinking, 'Why me?' It wasn't serving me any good. All it was doing was stealing my present. Then one day, something inside me snapped. It was a thunderclap moment that made me think, 'What's next?' I realized that I deserved to have a happy life too. I could sense my mindset shifting from 'Why me?' to 'What's next?' With this outlook, I wanted to actively seek ways to turn things around for myself.

Whether it's a whisper of self-compassion or a roar of determination, the realization that we can reclaim our happiness is deeply personal—and yet is a turning point we all share in our own unique way.

Over the next eighteen months, I tried multiple things. Some worked, but most failed. But I kept going back to it and kept trying. Whatever I explored, irrespective of the outcome, I found that it had a relationship to some common themes in life that cross our roads all the time. These themes are fundamental to our thoughts and outlook and shape the way we are. For example, how we define and understand success, what we learn from setbacks, what we associate our identities with, what constitutes our day-to-day decision-making, why we lose touch with our hobbies and interests as we grow, why we stop giving back to society, why we shy away from asking for help, what is our relationship with career, and last but not least, do we truly understand what freedom means, or do we take what influencers preach to us as truth?

I realized that my newfound views on the nine key life themes were instrumental in achieving my personal transformation. It is these life themes that will keep coming back to you now and then in life.

Was my situation unique? I am just an ordinary person. Like any other human being, my adversities are not unique. Most people face similar adversities in life, such as job loss, losing a loved one, a financial crisis, and bankruptcy in business. Inherently the adversities are not unique but the journeys are. It is the interaction and change in perspective that these life themes can bring to how we respond to these situations that make them unique. We look at the world through our lens. These themes will hopefully ensure that we have the right one.

If you are someone who is undergoing a difficult time, please remember that not going through it is not a choice, but how you choose to respond is something you can control. As I made the attempt to answer the numerous questions that I was juggling in my head, I realized that there exists one single idea for each of them—ideas and themes are designed by society to suit its collective personality. However, in chasing these collective notions, we tend to forget the most ancient wisdom in the world: Everyone is unique, and so will their ways be.

Life takes on a whole different meaning when we are aware, conscious and in dialogue with ourselves, and this is where these nine themes can help us craft our own transformation journey.

1. **Success:** We all understand success in our own ways. While there are many definitions by many philosophers and great personalities, we cannot deny that name, fame, money and power are the usual proxies. Can success be defined differently? Do people who strive

for success in a different way come out of FOMO (fear of missing out)? What could be a good framework for attaining success once you determine what success means to you?

2. **Setbacks:** These are a peculiar kind. A setback can happen to a David just as much as to a Goliath. Multiple setbacks can happen to the same person, one after the other or even at the same time. That's the nature of setbacks. Can we ever prepare for setbacks? What if we can develop a way to handle them? How should we create our coping mechanisms? A few scenarios will help us understand what really sets us back in life, some of them so grave that a comeback or moving on seems impossible.

3. **Identity:** What's the deal with identity? What is identity, and what does it constitute, and why does it come crumbling down in the event of a personal setback? Identity is one of the central elements of our existence. It is not about being famous, doing a great job or being popular. It is more fundamental and about how we look at ourselves and what gives us the confidence to go out each day and carry on with our lives.

4. **Decisions:** We all make numerous decisions every day: some immediate, some short-term and some long-term. Even not making a decision is a decision. I wanted to explore some key elements of decision-making that we knowingly or unknowingly bring to

our process. We all make decisions and sometimes our choices are not bound by a so-called rational framework.

5. **Hobbies:** Hobbies are an interesting life theme. If I were to ask you what your hobby is, many of us would fail to frame something in our minds, let alone pursue it in reality. The story was not the same when we were children. Our interests were diverse, and we seemed to have one thing that kept us engaged so much that we could almost go without food and water when into it. What happened along the way? How can a hobby help us in our lives? Is it too late to start something?

6. **Seeking help:** When dealing with adversity, all we want is a little help. But help doesn't come on its own; we have to work towards getting help. *We need to help ourselves to get help.* This is the change in perspective I want to share with my readers—a very powerful concept. I have explored sub-themes around why we feel shy asking for help, where help can come from, and why we should consider getting paid help from experts in the field.

7. **Relationship to career:** It is impossible to separate work and personal life. There are many fancy words, such as 'work–life integration', that try to convey the same meaning. Since work and life are two sides of the same coin, when discussing life themes, it is important to discuss our relationship with career. What do I mean by career? It could be a job; it could

be entrepreneurship or anything that helps us earn a living. In the post-COVID period, our relationship with career also underwent a change. No one can say for sure how it will further evolve. On the one hand, work-from-home versus work-from-office versus hybrid is hotly debated, and on the other hand, we have trends like the 'Great Resignation' and 'quiet quitting' at workplaces. So what does the new-age work expectation look like? We have to understand the scene and reflect to develop our own interaction mechanism.

8. **Giving back to society:** When was the last time you did something that did not directly benefit you? Many of us want to help the needy, raise our hands in support, and contribute to society, but somehow, we just do not know how. How to give back to society? Why does intention matter? Is it okay if I give money and not time? Are there any means by which I can contribute to society? Many questions arise as I reflect on this life theme.

9. **Freedom:** A very close theme to our hearts—we all want to be able to do the things that we want to do to feel *alive,* but due to a lot of factors in life, we end up doing things that help us *make a living*. Generally, when we talk about freedom, we tend to associate it with financial freedom, which gives us the ability to get up in the morning and decide what we want to do. If that's the case, then working professionals will

never have freedom. That is so unfair. While financial freedom is very critical, can there be more to it? What about freedom in our outlook, approach and daily lives? What should freedom look like?

Lastly, I want to address this question: What is the outcome of personal transformation? Most of us believe in and acknowledge a personal transformation when it leads to something spectacular. For example, a corporate employee quits job, founds a startup, and turns it into a unicorn. What if such a grand outcome does not materialize? Should we then say the personal transformation has not taken place? This is exactly the mindset we need to change. We need to view transformation as a process, the outcome of which is an awareness to better handle the situation that triggered it.

The purpose of this book is not to 'influence' but to share a point of view that my readers may find useful and can apply in their signature style to derive meaning and understanding about their lives. If the ideas presented serve as a solution or inspiration to even one person, then I believe the book would have served its purpose.

After my first book, *Work, Workmanship and Winning*, received so much love, appreciation and encouragement, I was quite pumped up about coming back to my readers with a second book. While *Work, Workmanship and Winning* is primarily about building an engaging and fulfilling career, *The Right Lens* is in many ways its spiritual successor that carries this question of fulfilment and engagement into everyday life.

The purpose and mission of this book are to inspire people to initiate their own personal transformation journey by interacting with the key life themes described and reflected upon in this book.

I would be extremely happy and grateful if you could send me your reflections on each chapter. To an author, this is the best recognition of his work. I can be contacted at ss@satyajitsenapati.com

1

Success

*'Success is not the key to happiness.
Happiness is the key to success.'*

—Albert Schweitzer

Everyone wants to be successful. Name, fame and money are the usual proxies. When we look at people who have great wealth and lead a life of comfort—whether we admit it or not—we feel a silent admiration. The same goes for people of renown and celebrities. We all look forward to getting that elusive selfie, that live meeting, and that coveted autograph with these successful people.

When you are successful, you will see that people strive for your attention and follow what you say and do. You seem to have some sort of authority and you feel that you are wanted, and this feeling is just great.

While this version and flavour of success is easy to recognize and emulate, it is important to understand how you want to define success for yourself. Is it this worldly success that you desire, or is it something else?

How Do We Define Success?

Many people have spoken about success. Authors, leaders and statesmen have shared their points of view and their definitions of success. There is a lot to learn from them. At the same time, it is important to reflect on this life theme and try to create a definition of success that works for us. After all, success is personal.

To begin with, let us see how we can define success. Well, there are two ways of doing this.

- First, what the world or society defines and accepts as the standard, and
- Second, what you think success means to you.

The world or society defines success in terms of tried-and-tested templates, such as jobs, business, academics, role models, etc. Each area has defined parameters of success, and the one who achieves or exceeds these parameters is declared the winner, and the rest of the world accepts and celebrates this victory. For example, cracking the IIT JEE entrance exam and getting into IITs is a standard template of success for students pursuing science courses and aspiring to be engineers. When a student does well in the entrance exam and gets admission to one of these coveted institutions, she or he is hailed as a success. The world applauds, and they get their moment of glory and limelight.

There is nothing wrong with this definition and understanding. In fact, it is the simplest way to define success.

Once you choose your template, it is a matter of following it until you meet the criteria. Students who choose civil services as a measure of their success have already accepted the template. All they now need to do is to work hard, prepare and hope to crack the exam. Some of them will make it to the most coveted jobs in India, but many will not.

When you accept a template, defining success is no longer a problem. The problem shifts to how to achieve the goal.

The second way is for you to define what success looks like for you personally. This is difficult to figure out and requires a lot of introspection.

It is an extremely personal choice that you have to make, the consequences of which you have to explain to no one. If you stop at any point on your transformation journey, you quit and consider something else. You can even go back to one of the tried-and-tested routes (if possible). You don't need to explain your choices to anyone. That is the beauty of it.

Many influencers and personalities today glorify a non-conventional option over a standard worldly option. For example, they glorify entrepreneurship more than a corporate job. Often the point of view is polarizing, and I don't endorse polarizing views. What is a good option for someone may not be a good option for another person. Hence, as I mentioned, the definition you choose for your success is personal, and you need not explain it to anyone.

What Are Your Success Goals?

An important step in defining success is to find out what your success goals are.

If I were to ask people what they would state as their success goals, the answer is invariably around financial and career aspects. Seldom is it about anything else.

The social environment plays a big role in shaping success goals. There was a time when finding a well-paying job and settling down was the ultimate face of success, and many people believed in it. While some continue to believe in the job story, today comparisons between jobs and entrepreneurship are common. While jobs are portrayed as being characterized by a lack of freedom, cutthroat competition, rat race, etc., entrepreneurship is celebrated as freedom, independence, and almost a panacea for all ills. In reality, it is a race everywhere—job or entrepreneurship. It is a question of which race you want to be a part of, and more importantly, how fast you want to run.

While defining success goals, don't be swayed by polarizing views; instead, always take a step back and think about what your real priorities in life are. To be able to do this, you need to clearly know what matters to you the most.

Success goals need not be just personal. It can be an ambition, a desire to impact humanity, or a personal goal that goes on to become a dream for others. Or it can be a mission that has nothing to do with what the world calls success. Let me give you three examples of success goals that are different from the traditional ones.

Wings to fly

Goals that transcend personal gains are not commonplace yet there are exceptions.

It was the mid-twentieth century, and the world was grappling with global hunger, a crises of epic proportions. In many parts of the developing world, particularly Asia and Latin America, famine and food shortages were rampant. Populations were growing at an unprecedented pace, but agricultural productivity lagged dangerously behind. The threat was imminent: without a solution, millions would face starvation.

At the forefront of this battle stood a man named Norman Borlaug, a scientist whose singular focus was to eradicate hunger by transforming the way humans grew food. Borlaug's vision wasn't just ambitious, it was revolutionary. He believed that feeding the world's growing population was not an insurmountable problem but one that could be solved with the right combination of science, perseverance and innovation.

Borlaug's breakthrough came in the 1940s while working in Mexico, where he developed high-yield, disease-resistant varieties of wheat. These new crops were more resilient, grew faster, and produced significantly higher yields. But he didn't stop there. He tirelessly promoted the use of modern farming techniques, including the strategic use of fertilizers, irrigation and crop management practices to maximize the potential of these new seeds.

In the 1960s, Borlaug's work was at the centre of a global movement that came to be known as the Green Revolution.

Countries like India and Pakistan, on the brink of famine, adopted his methods. Within a few years wheat production soared, helping these nations transition from food-importing to becoming self-sufficient. India, once synonymous with hunger, saw such a dramatic increase in grain production that it became an exporter of food.

The success goal Borlaug set himself was nothing short of monumental. Feeding billions required not just scientific ingenuity but also a relentless determination to overcome logistical, cultural and political barriers. Borlaug's goals had a deep sense of purpose and an unyielding belief in the power of science to serve humanity.

Imagine the scepticism he must have faced—trying to convince governments, farmers and institutions to adopt methods that seemed unconventional at the time. There were countless failures and moments of despair, but Borlaug's resilience never wavered.

It is estimated that his innovations saved over a billion lives from hunger and malnutrition, earning him the title 'The Man Who Saved a Billion Lives' and the Nobel Peace Prize in 1970. Norman's story is the story of an audacious success goal—one that transcends personal ambition and seeks to solve problems on a global scale.

While most of us set goals that are too personal and usually relate to what we wish to achieve, it is not easy to set impactful and ambitious goals. Sometimes it takes courage, discipline and an unwavering conviction to pursue such goals against all odds.

It was the second half of the 1800s and the early 1900s, and humankind was bracing for a miracle of sorts. Scientists were working on making humans fly. The aviation sector was seeing an unprecedented interest in this, and many scientists and researchers were singularly focused on one success goal—to make mankind fly.

On 17 December 1903, brothers Oliver and Wilbur Wright gave wings to this goal. They built the world's first aircraft, the Wright Flyer, making air travel possible for humans. They did not stop there and made further variations, improving their flying machines each time.

The success goal the Wright brothers set themselves was outrageously ambitious. Working towards such a goal—let alone realizing it—required great knowledge of engineering, and these two brothers were nothing if not self-taught (but brilliant) engineers. They spent years working in their workshop in Dayton, Ohio, building printing presses, bicycles, motors and other machinery. Their experience with bicycles was fundamental to the initial designs. Most aviation experts at the time had some connection to the bicycle industry.

Imagine the criticism and ridicule they would have faced every time they failed until they succeeded. Setting goals higher than self is no easy job.

The Quest for the Medal

One of the most apt examples of a success goal that starts as a personal goal and then goes on to become an inspiration for others comes from the field of sports: Karnam Malleswari, the first Indian woman to win a medal in weightlifting at the 2000 Olympics. Not just that, she became the first Indian weightlifter—male or female—to win a medal in the Olympics, and she was the only medallist for India in the 2000 Olympics.

Karnam was born in Andhra Pradesh and started showing interest in weightlifting and trained from the age of 12. Later she moved to Delhi, looking for better coaching facilities. She kept working on her skills and getting better at her craft. She married fellow weightlifter Rajesh Tyagi, and they settled in Haryana. In 2000, when she won the bronze medal for India, her victory was celebrated throughout the country. The Haryana government hailed this as the victory of its 'daughter-in-law'.

There is no doubt that behind Karnam's medal win there is a story of hard work, perseverance and a fight against all odds. But that's not what I want to convey with this little anecdote. The idea is to show how a personal success goal turned into inspiration for many. Karnam was hailed as a role model for women in Haryana. She seems to have broken the prevalent stereotypes around sports and women. Little did she know that this act of hers, her personal success goal, would directly or indirectly inspire women to take up and excel in sports such as weightlifting and wrestling, which are traditionally considered male sports. Today, Haryana is known to produce top female wrestlers such as Geeta Phogat, Babita Phogat, Vinesh Phogat and Sakshi Malik. A personal goal had indeed become a spark that ignited many minds.

The Alternate Perspective

Many unconventional areas in our lives can help us define our success goals but we overlook them. These areas are often ignored, or we do not give them much importance and take them for granted.

How many of us think of good parenting as a goal? How many of us define goals for our parents, society, helpfulness, etc.? How many of us set goals like 'today I will help two people in any way I can'? We usually take these things for granted as if they do not require any planning, thinking or attention. Can we also consider them success goals?

These kinds of goals are certainly not as attractive, as the end outcome is only known to you. But for some, it may be the most important goal to pursue.

Let's talk about a gentleman from my father's generation who had defined very unique success goals for himself. As a simple government employee, he owned only one house, unlike most of his peers, who had several houses. When he retired, he didn't have much savings left. Many of his peers considered him a failure as he could not amass worldly possessions and 'success' like they did. However, I never saw him unhappy about it. I asked him if he ever felt unhappy or considered himself unsuccessful. His response left me amazed:

> I have raised two good, well-cultured and respectful children. They are obedient and they love me. I gave them the best possible education within my means. Both of them are settled. Fortunately, my wife also supports

my outlook and has never demanded anything fancy in
life. We lead a simple life and are quite happy with it.

To me, he struck as a very successful man who defined his own success goals and is happy to live with them.

The most difficult aspect of choosing your definition of success is that the society-led and world-defined definitions of success are so ingrained that it is almost impossible for us not to accept them. Even if we find an alternate path, by choice or by force, the everlasting FOMO and clouded thoughts keep niggling in our minds. Many people have their own definition of success and do something different. When you do something different, there is chaos initially and then disruption before you find balance again. At these times you are constantly bombarded with what better things could have happened to you if you had stayed your course in the traditional path. So on this journey, there is a constant tussle between the unknown milestones of your chosen path versus the great things that could have happened to you if you had conformed to the worldly definition.

I remember one of the interviews I watched on YouTube where a well-known entrepreneur who had made it big talked about this aspect. As he narrated his story, he recalled how during his early days of entrepreneurship he often thought about his batchmates and friends who did exceedingly well in their corporate careers, and how his story could have been the same had he not quit his job to become an entrepreneur. Many a time, he had wanted to give up and look for a suitable job, not just because his startup had not taken off the way he had hoped but also because the path he had left behind sometimes seemed too lucrative, leading to FOMO. It is not uncommon for people to have this feeling when they want to try out something different from their usual routine.

Overcoming FOMO

The question is how we can overcome FOMO in a world where a comparison is waiting for us at every turn.

In my observation, people who have succeeded in finding their definition and overcoming FOMO have one thing in common. They somehow find meaning and purpose in what they do, a conviction in their chosen path, and the courage to stand by their thoughts. They believe that there is a reason greater than themselves for which they are doing this. The reason need not be to serve society or do charity; it could be a simple reason such as work–life balance for mental peace—a very personal reason. I know this is easier said than done, but the good news is that there are people who have done it, so there is no reason why others cannot do it too.

Building a Framework for Success

The road to success can be achieved through three simple but difficult-to-follow foundational building blocks:

1. Dream big, but start anyway
2. Work hard
3. Be patient

Building block 1: Dream big but start anyway

Many friends, philosophers and guides have time and again nudged us to think big. It is about the vision of how you want to confront or solve the challenge at hand. Often, when we face a problem and find a quick solution, we stop there. The solution might be a temporary fix, but we settle for it as we feel that we have solved the problem. Should our quest to search for a solution end at the first sight of a solution (even if it is not the best one)? Shouldn't we think BIG? Is solving the problem *completely* for ourselves big enough? Or can we go beyond it? Can you think BIGGER and solve it for others too?

If you can solve the problem for an entire population, the solution is bigger. Do not be satisfied with solving your personal problem—think bigger and on a large scale. If you face a problem and you are running from pillar to post to solve it, you can be rest assured that many others like you are going through a similar dilemma. Most will not even try, and adjust with the next best solution, while some will solve it on a personal level and not go beyond. 'Dream Big' is about finding a solution from the grassroots and looking at an opportunity to see if it needs to be solved for the community.

As an example of 'Dream Big', let's talk about what Bill Gates and Melinda French Gates did to combat world hunger.

Every year, millions of people suffer from a lack of food. The Gates Foundation worked relentlessly to help address this. It has donated more than $50 billion in endowments, received from various donors to this cause and other world problems.

The Foundation works with many NGOs and government bodies to fight hunger across the world, especially in African countries.

Bill Gates said in his essay 'The Future of Progress' in The Gates Foundation's 2022 Goalkeepers report:

> Hunger might not be a completely solvable problem. No one can reasonably promise that every one of the world's eight billion humans will always have enough to eat. But ensuring that sub-Saharan Africa and other low-income regions can feed their own people? That's a very achievable challenge, so long as the world changes how it approaches food crises.[1]

While raising food aid has been the primary means of finding a solution, factors such as climatic change that inhibit production and conflicts such as the Ukraine crisis increasingly point to the fact that hunger cannot be solved with humanitarian aid alone; it requires investments in agriculture, research and development, and innovation.

The true scale of 'Dream Big' lies in the realization that the problem must not only be solved, it needs to be eliminated. This will be possible when the humanitarian aid truly—at least in proportion—matches the investments in innovation in agriculture and production. 'Dream Big' is clearly seen and felt in the words of Bill Gates when he says:

---

[1] Gates, Bill, and Melinda French Gates, *The Future of Progress*, 2022, https://tinyurl.com/vyh9kxje. Accessed on 8 January 2024.

> *The goal should not simply be giving more food aid. It should be to ensure no aid is needed in the first place.*

Now that is a great example of 'Dream Big'. Create a situation where you do not have the problem in the first place.

Can just dreaming big help? Well, it is at least a start. However, most of the time when you dream big, you end up waiting for the stars to align, for things to fall into place, for the right moment, for the right people, etc. If you keep waiting, the 'Dream Big' remains just a dream. The essential step is to get started. Big steps or small, it does not matter; you just have to get started. I will share a personal anecdote here. When I started writing, I started thinking about my first book, but was not able to make much progress. I was waiting for all the thoughts to come together, for a proper structure to evolve in my mind, and believed that then I would start writing. Naturally, I could not make much headway with it, and frankly speaking, it was going nowhere. So I changed my style and pushed myself to take action and get started. I started writing at least one page regarding anything that interested me. This could be about an experience of the day or about something I could not do or get done that day. Nevertheless, I made progress. Eventually, when I started writing the book, these little steps helped.

Dream big and start anyway. You will eventually see things coming together and find yourself making efforts to move things.

Building block 2: Work hard

There is no substitute for hard work. It is said that genius is one per cent inspiration and 99 per cent perspiration. Although we know that hard work is required, we all want to be successful with little effort. People see success and believe it came overnight. However, it is almost impossible to see the 10x or maybe 100x failures behind each of these success crests. Every time there is a failure, it takes 2x the effort: 1x effort to get over the failure and 1x effort to start all over again. This happens to all successful people.

It is a popular belief that people who are born into success do not have to sweat it out. Even people with privilege must work hard because they are labelled successful only if they achieve more than their inheritance and legacy. The underprivileged must work hard because they have no entitlements and probably have to earn everything from scratch.

What does hard work mean? Does it mean 'boiling the ocean' or 'mining the earth'? Well, if you do that, the effort is too great. What we need to do is bark up the right tree and channel our efforts in a direction that is most likely to produce results. Often this is called 'smart working'. I prefer to call this 'intelligent working'. What is intelligent work and how does it complement hard work?

There was a consultant in our management consulting team in one of the companies that I worked for. We were part of a technology strategy group and consulted the chief information officers (CIOs) of large companies. We were based in India and expanding the core consulting team located in the United States. This consultant wanted to move from technology strategy to the business strategy and operations work area. However, transfers in MNCs are difficult. It happens when the company wants you to work and makes the changes, or if you put in a lot of time, patience and hard work to change your area of work. This consultant wanted to work in strategy and operations. He created a network map of partners working in strategy and operations. From this network map, he narrowed down the partners who worked with teams in India or at least expressed interest in working with teams in India. He then took the final list.

He crafted a value proposition statement showcasing his past work, education and interest in working in strategy and operations. He started reaching out to these partners, and there were twenty of them to reach out to. He didn't get the responses right away. After relentless pursuits and follow-ups, one partner agreed to give him some work. The work was not consulting work. It required him to compile three Excel sheets into one. He worked on it and delivered it. For the next three to six months, he worked on such assignments, editing and sometimes beautifying PowerPoints, doing some secondary research, etc. Towards the end of the fifth month, he got a call from this partner and was staffed into one of the projects. He travelled to the US for this project, which was for one of the largest beverage companies in the world. His 'intelligent work' ultimately paid off.

There are many things worth learning from this example:

- The meticulousness with which the consultant drew up the list of partners. He deliberately chose partners willing to work with the India team. Had he sent his email to all partners, it would have been a challenge to keep track, and it would have been a spray-and-pray approach that we should avoid.
- The diligence with which he wrote and followed up with each partner
- Even when he didn't get any response from most of them, he continued his efforts to connect and make them aware of what he could do.
- His willingness to do the work that probably didn't require much intellect. He continued to do small tasks until he got his big break.

Intelligent working is very critical as it gives direction to your hard work. Without the direction, hard work would be like boiling the ocean or mining the earth. All that you need can be accomplished with way less effort but only in the right direction.

Intelligent work = Hard work + Direction

Building block 3: Be patient

Patience is a great virtue. Many of us tend to expect results immediately when we work hard for something. It may or may not happen and largely depends on the task or objective you are trying to accomplish. The bigger the objective, the more time it will take, and more failures there will be before you hit the threshold.

Let's now read a brief story. Can you guess what it is about?

A boy learns on his eleventh birthday that he was actually born into the magical world of wizards and witches, and is the orphaned child of two powerful wizards. He then goes to enrol at a boarding school for wizards and thus begins his journey—making friends, having adventures, and finally defeating the villain.

You guessed it right. It's *Harry Potter* by J.K. Rowling. She wrote seven volumes of the famous series between 1997 and 2007. The impact of her work was such that the entire series sold over 500 million copies. It was also translated into at least 70 languages and has led to the creation of a global media franchise including films and video games.

When Rowling decided to publish the book, she was still relatively unknown at the time. The Christopher Little Literary Agency agreed to represent her. Then began a journey of rejections. Her book was submitted to 12 publishers and rejected by all 12 of them. Call it a stroke of luck: *Harry Potter* was picked up by Bloomsbury Publishing's children's literature department as Nigel Newton's eight-year-old daughter couldn't put the manuscript down after reading one chapter and wanted to keep on reading it.

It was such a powerful book that it spawned six sequels, and yet the first book in the series was rejected by 12 publishers. Imagine if Rowling had given up; if she had not had the patience to keep going, *Harry Potter* would not even have seen the light of day.

Let me give you a second example, not as great as J.K. Rowling's but from my life.

It is about my journey as a solopreneur. I was a corporate leader with close to two decades of work experience. As I progressed in the journey, I wrote my first book, *Work, Workmanship and Winning*. It received a tremendous response and was a number one bestseller on Amazon in the 'Workplace' category, which is usually dominated by foreign authors. The success opened up some opportunities for me in speaking engagements, workshops, etc. As I started getting more opportunities, I realized that my clients didn't know me enough, as my presence online and offline was not much. As a result, I couldn't progress as quickly as I had expected. Up until this point, I was a shy person on social media, but I soon realized building my social media presence was important. I started posting on LinkedIn, but most of my posts did not receive a large number of impressions and likes. The number of followers and connections I had was not great either. No matter how hard I tried, I was unable to crack the code of social media presence. Regardless of my success rate (or failure rate), I didn't give up. It took quite some time, but soon I started getting decent traction on my posts. Some of my posts even went viral, garnering views in millions. I started getting speaking engagements and workshops organically. I even started my mentorship programme. Slowly but surely, I started making progress, and it took a good 18 months. During this journey, I failed many times. There were many instances when the voices in my head said, '*This won't work*,' and many times

I even listened to them and almost gave up. But something inside kept telling me, *'Have patience'*, and I kept following this mantra. The big lesson here is that you may have a big dream, you may sweat it out by working hard, but if you don't have the patience, it is unlikely to work out for you.

A lack of patience makes us anxious and makes us give up on our goal. It makes us quit quicker—quicker than trying out other ways. Hence, patience is an extremely important aspect of achieving success. The most difficult part about this is that the lesson of patience is ever-continuing. Just when you think you have learnt a lesson or two in patience, a new scenario will emerge that will test you to a new level.

Measuring Success

If we have defined success goals and executed a plan to succeed, then we must also measure success. After all, what is the point of embarking on a journey if you don't know when or how to recognize that you've arrived?

Measuring success, if you conform to a worldly definition, is fairly straightforward. Success is simply attaining the said goal. In this sense, success means some kind of external validation—a medal, a promotion, a title, number of likes, subscribers, or any tangible marker that society readily acknowledges and celebrates. When you cannot do that, it is automatically deemed a failure. Not just by you, but also by the world around you. The parameters for success and failure are neatly laid out, leaving little room for ambiguity.

Measuring success when you define it in your own way is difficult. The process of measuring success becomes more nuanced and deeply personal. There are no universally accepted yardsticks, no applause from a crowd. Success in this sense is shaped by internal benchmarks, and these can be subtle and subjective and harder to articulate. There are a few indicators that can help in sizing up where you are on your journey. Let's make an attempt. The absence of regret or FOMO when you leave the known path is a critical indicator. It's the confidence to leave the well-trodden path behind without looking back enviously or second-guessing your choices. Instead, there is a quiet satisfaction in knowing that the path you've chosen aligns with your values and aspirations.

Feeling content with the choices you make and not having the urge to explain them to anyone is another critical indicator. It's about not feeling the need to explain or justify your choices to anyone. This freedom from external validation signifies that your success is truly your own.

The third indicator is a sense of purpose and fulfilment. It's waking up each day with a feeling of alignment, knowing that the work you do or the life you lead is contributing to something meaningful.

In a public appearance, actor-director Farhan Akhtar confessed to being disappointed with the outcome of his close-to-heart film *Lakshya*. He said that he had put in a lot of effort but the film didn't get a good box-office collection and was not successful. He also revealed why he made the film. Javed Akhtar, his father, had once visited an army establishment, and the officer there told him that despite all the praises about the Indian army, not many young people wanted to join it. Javed Akhtar wanted to make a film that addressed this issue. He wrote the story, and Farhan made the film. It was very close to their hearts.

But when the film was released, it was not a hit at the box office and was not commercially successful. Farhan was heartbroken. Thirteen years later, Farhan met an officer in Dehradun who praised him for the film. Farhan, still disappointed with the film's box-office performance, expressed his feelings. The officer told him to wait, turned to his soldiers, and asked, 'How many of you are here because of the impact of *Lakshya*?' To Farhan's surprise, about 70 per cent of them raised their hands. Imagine the goosebumps Farhan would have felt.

We often measure success by metrics like money, fame and reach. It's natural to use these as proxies. But sometimes in our focus on these metrics, we forget the original purpose of our work. Wasn't *Lakshya*'s true success in its ability to inspire young people to join the army? Wasn't that the purpose? When we measure success, perhaps we should look at purpose and impact above all. Money and fame can certainly be a measure of success but the real question is: Does your impact align with your purpose?

The beauty—and challenge—of measuring success this way is that only you can truly assess it. It requires introspection and self-awareness to identify what really matters to you, and the courage to stick with it, even when the world may not applaud or even understand your journey. Ultimately, the true measure of success is not in how others perceive your life, it is how fulfilled you feel living it.

An Inclusive View of Success

After defining how to measure success, there is a final point I want to address in this chapter—what should your outlook toward success be?

While much of the chapter talks about success through the choices you make, I want to augment the thoughts.

When we view success either through societal norms or through a personal lens, we are still, in some sense, 'rigid' in our perspective. We may fixate on one decision and dismiss others as invalid or unworthy. This rigidity can limit our growth and understanding, reducing success to a narrow, binary concept, irrespective of the lens.

The true outlook of success should be 'inclusive'. What does that mean? To me, an inclusive outlook for success acknowledges and respects the diverse ways in which success can manifest itself. I may still prefer one definition over the other, but I also recognize and acknowledge the other kind of success. A right view of success means a sense of achievement for self and respect for what others have achieved. For instance, someone whose definition of success is wealth creation may admire the selfless contributions of a social reformer, while a person dedicated to public service might respect the entrepreneurial spirit of a business leader. Inclusivity allows us to celebrate the diversity of aspirations and achievements without devaluing our own.

It is also important to understand and appreciate that failures are not absolute. An inclusive view of success does not see failure as the opposite of success but as an integral part of the journey. An inclusive view encourages us to define success not only by external outcomes but also by the richness of our experiences, the depth of our relationships, and the meaning we find in our endeavours. If we can develop this view of success, we will be able to appreciate that success is not a zero-sum game but a collective celebration of efforts, resilience and purpose.

2

Setbacks

'Champions keep playing until they get it right.'

—Billie Jean King

Life is long. Lots of things happen. We meet many people, some we form lifelong bonds with, and others just pass by. We go through many events—great ones, not-so-good ones, and yes, setbacks.

Setbacks are events in life that put you in situations where you do not know how to move forward. Setbacks can occur in both personal and professional lives. Mind you, they are not mutually exclusive, which means both personal and professional setbacks can happen to the same person at the same time over and over again.

Setbacks have the potential to scar you for life. That is why it is important to deal with setbacks, find appropriate closure and move on. People often confuse difficult times with setbacks. But setbacks are much more profound. They take you to the dark by-lanes where it is difficult to find the direction you must tread.

In my endeavour to reflect on setbacks, I would like to discuss four different scenarios or setbacks that can occur in one's life. These are just four scenarios. There can be many others that are personal and specific to an individual. The point is that through these examples I want to build a generic model for living through setbacks.

Job Loss, Layoffs and Setbacks in Professional Life

Job loss, layoffs and professional setbacks are the most common forms of career setbacks. It can happen to anyone, yes, anyone—a David as well as a Goliath.

While my focus for this section will remain on job loss, setbacks can happen in any profession. In the film industry, for example, a new actor makes it big after his debut movie only to experience a slump in which his movies flop one after the other. A cricketer who is the hottest talent to watch out for suddenly loses form and goes through a bad patch and is almost dropped from the team. In any field or profession, setbacks can happen, and no field or profession can be immune to them. It takes a lot of courage, determination, hard work, a positive frame of mind, and luck to get back to your former best or do better. The world is full of such examples.

Setbacks bring their trials, along with prejudices and stigmatization. Let me talk about an incident that spells out a common and deep-rooted prejudice against people who are laid off: the lack-of-performance prejudice. I distinctly remember some of my friends sitting at a friend's house and talking about one of our friends who was sacked due to cost-cutting in the company. My friend's uncle (at whose place we were) overheard us and almost immediately said, 'He must have underperformed at work. Otherwise why would you ask someone to leave?' Such is the level of bias people carry towards job loss that every time they hear someone was laid off, they conclude that it is because the person was a poor performer. This is why it is not surprising to see the reaction of a person who is fired—they try to hide it from others. In this case, we knew for a fact that our friend was not laid off over bad performance, but as part of a mass layoff due to cost-cutting. We tried to tell this to my uncle too, but it was not worth explaining this to someone who already had a strong point of view on the subject.

Thankfully things are changing, and more and more people are talking openly about such situations and embracing a more open mindset, but a large number of people still suffer from the age-old prejudice.

Nevertheless, the basic rule for layoffs is: From an employer's perspective, no one is indispensable. Nowadays, we hear about layoffs practically all the time. You would know of startups and large conglomerates alike carrying out mass layoffs. There are two dimensions to layoffs. The first dimension concerns the reason someone is fired, and the second dimension is the career level at which the job loss occurs and its consequences.

The reason dimension

Layoffs are triggered due to various reasons. The most common reason is a dwindling economy. Every time there is an economic slump, slowdown or downturn, mass layoffs are the first thing you hear about. This happened on a grand scale in 2008. Since then, every time there is an economic slump or the signs of it, you hear about mass layoffs.

An economic downturn is not the only reason for mass layoffs. Sometimes a company bites off more than it can chew in its growth plan. For example, many startups indiscriminately hire people given the valuation, growth, etc. The investors then back out for whatever reason, and the company is left with 'extra flab'. The only logical way to get rid of them is in the form of a mass layoff. The newspapers and social media are full of such news and stories.

A third reason for layoffs is neither related to the economy nor to the company's ill-conceived growth plan. It is the employees not getting along with their bosses. While it is common in the case of a family-run business, it also occurs in a professionally managed multinational with mature HR practices. However, these are not mass layoffs but individual cases.

A fourth reason is when a company decides to wind up operations in a particular geography. This is usually related to economic slumps. However, it could also be that the company is not profitable or competitive in that region or country and hence ceases operations.

A fifth reason pertains to the employee's attitude, behaviour, misconduct and performance. These are shortcomings in the employee's professional quotient—the overall integration of skills, competencies, behaviour and attitude of the employee. Professionals need to be aware of their shortcomings. Until they acknowledge these lacunae, these issues will keep coming back irrespective of the job.

Sometimes new technology comes along, and this brings a wave of layoffs. Generative AI (ChatGPT et al.) is one such wave. This is the sixth reason why mass layoffs can happen.

While there are many more reasons that we can talk about, the six reasons for layoffs that I mentioned are more prevalent.

The career-level dimension

The second dimension is the career level at which job loss can occur. This could be entry-level, mid-level or leadership. Only the context and the consequences are different. Let us examine these in terms of financial aspects and job opportunities.

Entry level

At the entry level, layoffs generally occur en masse. For example, you hear news that company X has laid off 10,000 people and company Y has laid off 19,000 people, etc.

- **Financial aspects:** At this stage, the family responsibilities that you carry on your shoulders are less (except if you are the breadwinner). At the same time, you do not have enough savings. That's the trade-off.

- **Job opportunities:** It is well known that professional career opportunities follow the pyramid framework. This means more jobs at the entry level. Yes, that's good news. Finding another job should take six months on average.

Mid-level

The layoffs are generally en masse again, but a little less in number. You hear the news that company X has fired 400 people and company Y has laid off 800 people, etc.

- **Financial aspects:** At this stage, the family responsibilities on your shoulders increase as you may be married and may have children and EMIs. However, the silver lining is that you may also have saved some money, which can help buy you a bigger runway before your next launch.
- **Job opportunities:** At this stage, the chances of finding a job are a little less than at entry level. However, the good news is that your compensation is also in an acceptable range. Hence, chances are good that you will land yourself a job in twelve months.

Leadership

Leaders too face layoffs. Only the number of layoffs is not high enough to get any spicy news headlines. In fact, the higher the position, the more you come under the line of fire, and your firing may not always be linked to economic reasons.

- **Financial aspects:** You would have saved money. This can help you stay afloat for a relatively longer period.
- **Job opportunities:** The opportunities will be very few. Your current compensation would be high, and you would also be on the wrong side of the age-o-meter (corporate-invented meter to measure your usefulness with respect to your age and compensation). Couple this with the fact that leadership roles are far and few in companies. All this makes it difficult to get a shot again at a similar position. At the leadership level, it can take a couple of years to get something relevant.

No matter the reason or career level, a layoff is a big career setback.

There is a cycle that you go through when you are laid off.

The initiation

This is the phase in which you receive the information and take time to process it. If it is a sudden layoff, there is not much you can do. However, if it is a notice layoff, you run pillar to post to make things work—another project, a department change, and finding a new job within the notice period.

The day

This is the day when you get laid off and officially taken off the payroll. You feel a certain lightness and a feeling of being unchained and free.

Post-separation

The first few days (or months) feel like a welcome break. You no longer have to get up on time, follow a robotic routine, and end your day. You seem to have complete control over your time, and you realize how tight things were back when you still had your job. In these times, you also look for jobs and do not compromise on the role or salary, believing you will find a job pretty soon.

Job loss is still a taboo. Especially for folks coming from small towns, there is a lot of worry about what people will think at the place where their parents live. Thus begins a phase of 'hiding the job loss'. You don't talk much about the office anymore (something which took up almost 80 per cent of your conversations earlier). You try hard to find work and escape this ordeal—get a job before anyone knows that you have been laid off. However, nothing seems to be working. No interview calls, and when calls do come, they don't lead to an offer. In short, you are going through a slump.

Months go by, and you still do not have a breakthrough. You start thinking about doing something on your own. This takes money, resources, and an environment that you may not be able to pull together. You continue your search. Your ego is battered, your identity lost, your self-respect at an all-time low, your self-confidence has gone out the window—all this can happen to you.

Finally, one day, you convert an opportunity. You land a job. It may or may not be the best, but it's a fresh start, and you take it, and life gets back on track. This is the happy path. Another happy path is for people who figure out self-employment—either through freelancing or entrepreneurship.

There are also sad paths where the wait goes on for years. I know a friend who was laid off and continued looking for a job and finally found a job after two years, and whatever he tried in between, he wasn't just able to make it happen.

Victory

What does victory look like? Getting back to the workforce or doing something of your own?

Absolutely not. There is no guarantee that this unfortunate event will not happen again. There will be economic slumps, companies will mess up growth plans, you may not get along with your boss again, companies may shut shops, and your 'something of your own' might fail. What does victory look like then? Here is what I think victory or success should look like coming out of this setback:

- This setback can happen again.
- Layoffs do not happen just because someone is underperforming. Layoffs can happen even to the best of the best.
- You failed to demonstrate the openness about job loss that you had advocated. You hid this for months so that you would get your next job before anyone found out. By no longer endorsing this view, you understand your responsibility to make others feel comfortable around you when they face job loss.

- During your layoff period, you realize some of the finer aspects of life. You understand what work–life balance should look like for you.
- You value things more than what you previously used to.
- You need to keep in mind that not everyone you ask for help will extend it. Some would like to help but may not be able to due to their obligations. Have no hard feelings for them.
- You understand that when someone approaches you for help, you should do your best.
- Influencers today are vocal about self-employment, entrepreneurship and financial independence. These are great, but don't be swayed by opinions. Understand what works for you. It is important to decide which race you want to be in, but most importantly, decide how fast you want to run.
- Once back in a job, you have a different outlook on work and life. You treat people with empathy; you are more connected with your family, and most importantly, with yourself.

If you, my friend, can achieve this victory after coming out of a layoff, you have learnt a valuable life lesson. As they say, there is a price to everything; consider the lack of income during this period as the tuition fee for one of the biggest learning phases of your life.

An Unexpected Loss

Let me narrate an interesting incident from one of the greatest epics—the Mahabharata. The incident illustrates the *maya* (illusion) that surrounds life.

After losing a game of dice, the Pandavas were to spend twelve years in the forest and one year incognito. If they are found during this period, they must live another thirteen years in exile. One day while wandering in the forest, the Pandavas felt thirsty. The youngest of them, Sahadev, climbed a tree and discovered a pond nearby. Asking his brothers to rest, he made his way to the pond. When he got there and was about to drink the water, he heard a voice warning him not to do that without answering his questions. Sahadev was extremely tired and thirsty. He paid no attention and went on to drink the water. At that moment, the voice of Yaksha, the protector of the pond, killed him. Since Sahadev didn't return, Yudhishthira became impatient and sent Nakul after him. Nakul also met the same fate. He was followed by Arjun and Bhima, who met the same fate. When finally Yudhishthira arrived at the pond, he saw the bodies of his brothers, and the voice told him the same thing. Instead of drinking water from the pond, he agreed to answer Yaksha's questions. Yaksha asked him 126 questions, and Yudhishthira gave satisfactory answers to all. One of the questions that Yaksha asked was, 'What is the greatest paradox that baffles the world?' Yudhishthira replied, 'Every person knows that death is the ultimate truth of life, yet he continues to think that it is not his ultimate truth.'

Impressed by his answers, Yaksha gave back the lives of all his brothers. Yaksha was Yama testing the righteousness of Yudhishthira.

The point here is we all know that we are mortal. That whoever breathes shall one day breathe their last. Yet, we go about our daily chores as if nothing will ever happen. We believe that our loved ones will never die, that we will never die. So when a loved one dies suddenly, our whole world comes to a standstill. While losing a loved one is always heart-shattering, the situation is a little different when the loved one is terminally ill—a process through which we prepare for the final departure. When death comes suddenly, we don't understand what has happened, what has hit us, and how we should react.

In recent years, as COVID wreaked havoc, families were wiped off as if they never existed. Many families experienced the sudden demise of their loved ones, which only compounded the grief because one did not have the opportunity to share their grief due to COVID-19 norms.

I went through just such a sudden loss. I came home to Bhubaneswar after two years to spend some quality time with my parents. When I reached Bhubaneswar, we all fell ill with COVID within a fortnight. My mother had the worst infection. Within days, her oxygen levels dropped, and she was admitted to intensive care. A day later we were told that she was recovering, and that same afternoon we received a call from the hospital that she had died after suffering a cardiac arrest. This was a big blow, as we were planning to bring her home. She was recovering, and then this happened. Within two days, my world turned upside down. I didn't know how to react. I was suffering from COVID myself. I had a chest infection and was about to be hospitalized. It was the peak of the second wave of the pandemic, and I performed the last rites on the cremation ground wearing a hazmat suit. It was the most difficult and testing time for my family.

Like any setback, this one also has a process. The person experiencing grief goes through phases, and if they are lucky, there is a new definition of victory with which they emerge.

The denial

This is the first phase. Although you know that the event has happened, you do not want to acknowledge it. You believe that your loved one will come back, and things will return to normal again. But all along you know that this isn't going to happen, and yet you keep denying this truth of our lives.

Anger

When you lose a loved one, there is a lot of anger that follows. You get angry thinking that the person did not receive the right medical treatment, that they probably would have survived if you had taken them to another hospital. You wish you could spend more time with them. And above all, some of us also get angry at God.

Acceptance and making peace

After a while, you realize the harsh reality, accept the loss and make peace with it. There is a general perception that if you show your feelings, for example through tears, you are considered weak. You are labelled as soft. In reality, it is the other way around. People who show emotions are those who recognize their own emotions very well. They have a high emotional quotient (EQ). The first step to healing from a personal loss is always to acknowledge what you are feeling. Only then can you make peace with the situation.

Victory

What does victory look like in this case? When we go through a personal tragedy, many things change within us. There is a lot that we start seeing clearly. When a loved one who stood by your side dies, as opposed to the numerous acquaintances you would have made in your life, you begin to see the difference.

- You accept reality and make peace. It is said that happiness increases and sadness decreases when you share it with others. One of the ways that helps immensely with acceptance and making peace is sharing your feelings with people who genuinely care for you.
- A lot of people will advise you to move on. However, this is not so easy. We never move on; we just push ourselves to go with the flow, and this is done by looking at the future.
- Older people and middle-aged members of the family look forward to the next generation. Younger people

look forward to their life ahead. That's how moving on is done.
- You are more compassionate and empathetic when it comes to loss.
- You know what to do when someone loses his or her loved one. It is not about crying and wailing with them. It is about taking the step to help them accept and make peace. You will not be able to immediately extend this act of kindness, responsibility and compassion. Sometimes it may take a year or more to develop this empathy.
- Understand that this is the process and this can happen again and again. I lost my father-in-law in 2022 after losing my mother to COVID in 2021. So personal losses can happen over and over again even if you have not recovered from one yet.

When a personal loss occurs, it is not about whether you can move forward. Everyone will eventually get out of it. It is more about should a personal loss like this make you bitter or make you more empathetic, or would you just go back to your old way of being indifferent? The answer to this is the right definition of victory.

Surviving Medical Setbacks

When we are hale and hearty, everything looks rosy. Only when you are healthy can you take care of your responsibilities and perform your duties. Otherwise, every task looks daunting

The British tennis player Sir Andrew Barron Murray OBE, better known as Andy Murray, played in the era of the Big Four—Roger Federer, Rafael Nadal, Novak Djokovic and himself. He won three Grand Slam singles titles, two at Wimbledon and one at the US Open, and was ranked the No.1 player in the world for 41 weeks according to the Association of Tennis Professionals (ATP). He has also won gold at the Olympics and won a total of 41 titles—a career that few can dream of having, let alone achieve.

In addition to Andy's illustrious career, there is one more aspect of his life that has been the subject of much discussion—his long streak of injuries. Andy had to drop out of the 2013 French Open due to his hip injury. After a four-week break, he was back in action. However, after being forced to withdraw from the 2013 French Open, the injury recurred during the US Open and later during the Davis Cup World Group play-offs. The injury got worse and worse, and Andy decided that surgery was the best way to fix the problem. After the surgery, he continued to play, winning many tournaments and rising to the world No.1 ranking.

In 2017, Andy suffered an elbow injury that put him out of action for more than a month. Later that year, a persistent hip injury kept him out of action for most of the time, which also led to a slump in the rankings.

A year later, in 2018, Andy underwent hip surgery, which put him out of action for a long time as he embarked on a long, arduous journey to recovery. He played games in between, but most of the time it was a battle between fitness and injury.

In 2019, plagued by a hip injury, an emotional Andy announced in a press conference that he might retire from professional tennis due to injuries, particularly his hip injury. He said that he suffered from hip pain in his daily activities and even mundane tasks such as putting on his shoes and socks were painful. He talked about the possibility of a second hip surgery but wasn't sure if it could prolong his career. In his own words, the surgery could give him a 'better quality of life and relieve him of the pain.' Imagine the pain this sportsman may have felt that caused him to give up the game he loved so dearly and defined his identity.

He eventually underwent the Birmingham hip resurfacing (BHR) surgery developed as an alternative to total hip replacement (THR). After the initial recovery, Andy said he was pain-free but did not want to rush his comeback and decided he would start playing doubles to test his readiness.

By 2022, Andy was back playing professional tennis in singles and winning at that too. He broke into the top 50 of the world rankings. In 2023, Andy played the longest match of his career against Thanasi Kokkinakis, which lasted five hours and 45 minutes.

Andy's struggle and triumph is one of the most inspiring stories of our time, speaking volumes about mental strength and hope and a battle against a health-related setback—something that could have ended his career forever.

While Andy's exemplary recovery is a story of celebrities, there are also stories of ordinary people.

My friend is currently in a situation where his health, or

rather his illness, is a setback for the whole family. A few years ago, he was diagnosed with a specific case of autoimmune disease. There are more than 80 types of autoimmune diseases that affect a wide range of body parts. In his case, he was practically unable to move and could therefore no longer go to work. Despite the degree of seriousness, he is unable to work from home either. He has two children who still go to school. When he was confronted with this setback in his life, he simply didn't know what to do. The loss of income, managing household expenses, and the children's education—life almost came to a standstill.

Luckily a friend came to his rescue. He helped him assess his savings and assets and discovered that he was falling short of a few thousand rupees a month. He then mobilized crowdfunding. A few agreed, and thanks to their contribution, life seems to be getting back on track. In a few years, I'm sure his children will be grown up and have jobs, and soon the household will be on its feet.

Victory

What does victory look like here? The family is now getting financial support. So in this case, victory is:

- My friend's resolve to exhaust all possibilities to support his family with the savings and assets he has.
- His sense of gratitude to the small group of people who are helping him.

- His friendship with the person helping him in this time of need.
- Most importantly, he believed that it is only a matter of time before his children grow up and take charge of things.

Dealing with Health Setback of Family Members

For much of my career, I have stayed away from my hometown, Bhubaneswar. However, I ensured I visited at least twice a year. Whenever we have a family function or get-together in my hometown, a certain family friend (from my father's generation) always turns up. He always has a smile on his face and radiates tremendous warmth when I meet and greet him. I recently visited him at his home. I knew that his wife was unwell and that his son, who has had mental health problems since childhood, also lived with them. When I met him at his house, he greeted me with his usual warm smile. After the usual exchanges, I sat down with him and started a conversation. He wanted to get some snacks for me. I resisted as I was not hungry. In due course, I learnt that his wife had been bedridden for five years. Although she was not terminally ill, her body was not strong enough for her to get back on her feet. She had developed bedsores, and due to ageing, she had cataracts in both eyes. It was almost certain that she would not recover and would remain bedridden for the rest of her life. I met his son, who was then fifty years old. Due to his mental health issues, which he has had since childhood, he was pretty much restricted to his home and only interacted with his parents. His mother didn't speak much and no longer recognized people, as cataracts had blurred her vision. Despite this situation, Uncle always had a smile on his face. He got up to make me some tea. I helped him and made tea for both of us. We sat down and talked about a lot of things, from books to startups. He gave me a few suggestions, and then I got up to leave. As we said our goodbyes, he smiled again and said, 'Why don't you come around again sometime, and we can have lunch or dinner together? I couldn't offer anything today.'

I was very moved after this visit. I just didn't know how to react. We get so disturbed and stressed when little things inconvenience us, and yet here is a man who struggles with this dual challenge of wife and son and is yet all smiles, caring and concerned. He fulfils all duties with a smile and shows up at every family function without fail, and if you meet him without knowing this background, you will never know what he is going through. The grit is undeniable, and the way he approaches everything in life is inspiring. Amidst these difficult life scenarios, he has a little ritual of his own. He gets up in the morning, goes for a walk, goes to the nearby greengrocer, buys vegetables, goes to the nearby sweet shop, eats a sweet, and comes back. Perhaps this is his 'me time', something that recharges his batteries so that he can face his struggles every day with a smile on his face.

Victory

It is extremely difficult to fathom what challenges and difficulties the person in front of you is facing, especially if they are all smiles. In such cases, victory may look like:

- The ability to keep smiling and get back to the fight every day.
- The ability to stay calm and be a caregiver.
- The ability not to complain but to accept and move on.
- A strong sense of duty and obligation.
- The ability to not turn bitter. The question is whether you can still find your own little space where you can spend time in solitude and peace.

Generic Framework for Handling Setbacks

Once a king called upon all his wise men and asked them, 'Is there a single sentence, a single piece of advice, or a single suggestion that works in joy and sorrow, in defeat and victory? In difficulties and in easy times? One answer that works for all situations and circumstances?'

All the wise men were baffled, scratching their heads. After all, the king had asked a question, and they had to answer. They sent people in all directions to gather information and talk to sages. After analysing all the data, insights and information and discussing them in detail, they returned to the king and presented their answer to him.

The message was: 'THIS TOO SHALL PASS'.

In life or in career, no matter what the circumstances, this too shall pass. Neither the good times last forever nor can the difficulties last forever. Have faith, and this too shall pass.

When you are confronted with a setback, not getting through it is not an option, but how you respond to it is a choice.

Try to follow these steps. In the end, it is all about keeping up your efforts.

1. Accept your condition. The more you are in denial, the more difficult it will be.
2. Ask for help but remember that very few people will help you. Those who don't, do not keep any grudge for them in your heart.
3. Keep trying. Either the setback will turn into something beautiful, or you will develop the strength to live with it and endure it.
4. Understand that this too shall pass. Nothing is permanent. Even our time on this planet is temporary.

To summarize, I discussed four setback scenarios. Are they exhaustive? Absolutely not. There will be many types of setbacks, more in your personal life than in your professional life. The point is to understand that setbacks can happen to anyone, at any time, and any number of times. The least we can do as humans is:

- Disassociate our biases towards a person's setbacks. For example, if someone loses their job, they are not necessarily an underperformer, or if someone is

smiling and going about their business, it doesn't mean they might not be going through hell.
- Quit the judgement and not let our prejudices get the best of us.
- Be compassionate and empathetic, and help people. Help genuinely and not just as a formality.
- Redefine victory for yourself. Not based on the success of the outcome but based on the transformation that the setback can trigger in you.

As the saying goes, 'this too shall pass'. Setbacks will also pass. And if they don't, then at least we develop the strength to get through them and live with them.

3

Identity: Who Am I?

*'You are not a drop in the ocean.
You are the entire ocean in a drop.'*

—Rumi

A dear friend of mine was an accomplished marketer in one of the well-funded startups in India. He was doing well and looked like he could do this job well. Tragedy struck in the form of a layoff. Due to cost-cutting measures during the COVID-19 pandemic, he was asked to leave the company along with many others. He continued his job search, but jobs at his level didn't come by easily. He kept looking. When I met him, I couldn't believe he was still the same man who used to be so jolly and happy. It had been six months, and he wasn't able to find a new job. He fell into pessimism, his self-confidence began to wane, and he rarely smiled. His health had also deteriorated due to the stress and anxiety of unemployment. Naturally I was concerned, and in a heart-to-heart conversation, he revealed that losing his job was very hard for him. It made him feel like he had lost his identity.

His words hit me hard and made me think. I felt that we tie our identity to our job and work so intensely that we don't seem to exist without it. It's like a company health insurance that ceases to exist when we are no longer in one company and begins again when we work for another. *What we do for a living seems to be the only thing that defines our identity.* This raised the question of what constitutes our identity, and I deemed it prudent to explore this further.

In Search of Identity

Tell me about yourself. For most of us, the answer to this question is most likely our identity at that stage. Some of us will go on talking about our professional resumes, others about our roles such as a working mother, a stay-at-home father, etc. Whatever it may be, when we are confronted with such a question, the answer defines our identity at any given point in time. Moreover, the answer to this question changes over time. Identity is therefore not static but evolves based on various factors in life. It is a constantly changing process and a continuous one.

So what is identity? Of course, by now you would have realized that it is not a specific dimension. What is it then? I went on a search and spoke to different people from different regions, age groups, professions, genders and economic backgrounds. The findings were a revelation. The insight helped me to define what constitutes the concept of identity and the key elements that shape it. I found that while some elements are part of who we are and we don't have much choice about them, some elements connect to our identity as we embark on the journey of life. Some are obvious, while others, although important, are conveniently ignored or we are not aware of.

Work, job et al.

When we spend a long time doing something—a business, studies, sports—this 'something' takes over our identity. For example, when we study we identify ourselves as students. Apart from being students, we also associate our identity with everything we do outside the curriculum or as a hobby. For example, 'I am not only a student but also a good badminton player, a good painter, a singer, etc.'

When we join a job, our professional life becomes our identity. We tend to talk more about our work, where we work, what we do, etc., and that makes up our identity. The story is the same whether you are a working professional or an entrepreneur. Whatever we do (or are most active in) becomes our identity.

Perhaps the most interesting elaboration of our professional identities can be found on LinkedIn, where we can see how people portray themselves in various creative ways.

- Some people limit themselves to what they do for a living, that is, their job titles.
- Some people stress pronouns that identify them, such as he or she, she or their, etc.
- Some highlight their professional identity, such as coach, author or mentor.

- Some like to talk about their life philosophies, such as being a minimalist, an optimist, etc.
- Many list all the companies they have worked for, especially the big companies, stating ex-Google, ex-Facebook, etc.
- Some write phrases that reflect what they do.
- Many write their success as a tagline, such as 'bestselling author'.

Nonetheless, every representation is a way we identify with ourselves in the online space and life. We want others to identify with us. It is our professional online persona.

In general, we are so devoted to this aspect of our lives that for many it is our sole identity. So imagine feeling like you've lost your identity when it's ripped away from you, as was the case for my dear friend. Despite knowing that it is only a part of life, attaching identity to 'what we do' is deeply rooted.

Where we come from

When we meet people at a gathering, most of us tend to hold back. Typically, we don't make the first move. We only introduce ourselves when necessary. However, some of us are more loquacious and take the initiative to talk to people. When we talk to a stranger, we introduce our name and maybe mention a bit about our profession. But when we meet people with whom we have something in common, the process of going back in time begins. Invariably, if two people from the same city, village or town meet at another place, they are sure to talk about the things that bind them together. They start by identifying where the other person's house is in their hometown. This is followed by some common places, people, habits and behaviours. Nevertheless, where you come from is also part of your identity.

I had an interesting conversation with a co-worker that may give a different impression of this concept. When I started a new job in Mumbai, I met someone at work, and while we were both taking a coffee break and having a casual conversation, he asked me where I was before Mumbai.

I said, 'Bangalore', and his eyes lit up because he still had family in Bengaluru and hadn't quite moved to Mumbai yet.

I then asked him which part of Bengaluru. He replied, 'Marathahalli!' At this point, it got exciting because I lived there too. As we narrowed down on areas, we discovered that we lived in different blocks of the same apartment complex. What an amazing coincidence!

It is not just the place you come from; the place where you have spent your time also becomes a part of your identity as you pick up many stories, behaviours and characteristics.

Family and social circle

Your family and your social circle are a big part of your identity. Who are you? A son or daughter, a brother or sister, a father or mother, a dear friend—all these are elements of your identity.

You didn't choose your parents; they were chosen by God, and by and large we all have the best parents God could have chosen for us.

As far as the spouse is concerned, there is this old adage:

Marriages are made in heaven. Nevertheless, a successful partnership here (as with any other partnership) depends on two important factors: finding the right person and being the right person for the partnership.

Friends come in all shapes and sizes, and each one plays a different role and completes you differently: *Har ek friend zaroori hota hai* (It is important to have all kinds of friends). Some friends have a good influence on you; others lead you down the forbidden path. Nevertheless, you can learn something either way.

We talk so much about work–life balance, the importance of family, being with friends, and so on. However, we don't give due importance to this aspect of our identity as much as we give to our job or profession. Pause for a moment and think about how much you invest in this aspect of your identity in today's hectic world. Consider how we wish our dear friends a happy birthday. Don't we wish most of our friends happy birthday via WhatsApp or Facebook? I am not being cynical here and saying that social media has destroyed our social skills (that's debatable ☺). But I suggest the next time a friend's birthday is coming up, just pick up the phone and call them; trust me, you will feel much more connected than the ticking off we do via SMS or WhatsApp.

Successful people invariably have a better work–life balance. They are very deeply connected to their inner circle. So if busyness is a reason, then it is an excuse and nothing more.

In the early days of my professional career, every time my mother called me during office hours, I would hurriedly respond with a quick 'yes' or 'no' and hang up. I would promise her that I would call her in the evening. Sure enough I called, but at that point, I had no energy left after a long day, and it was only a brief conversation. Is this relatable?

Over time, my parents got older. After my mother passed away, I always regretted the curt yes or no over the phone, the lack of photographs capturing our moments together, and many other small things. I wish I had been more present.

Parents don't get any younger, and eventually the inevitable will happen. All I am trying to do with my father is to be more present and mindful.

Our jobs and professions might require us to be away from our parents, and we may be very busy. Even if that is the case, we can be patient, mindful and present.

Families and social circles are big parts of your identity. The question is whether you acknowledge the importance of this element.

Value system: Religion, faith and spiritualism

Religion plays a significant role in one's identity. If there is any component besides 'what we do' that is important to one's identity, it is religion. Religion is linked to faith and is instrumental in defining the core set of values. We do not decide which religion we are born into, but we sure consider it our duty to follow the practices. These practices enter our routine from childhood, shape our outlook, and become our way of life. This way of living defines our identity.

Faith and spiritualism are closely related concepts.

Religion is closely related to faith and can be instrumental in defining core values that guide life choices. However, faith and spiritualism go beyond religion; they are universal tools that help us connect with ourselves and the world around us. Our values determine our behaviour, decision-making and priorities, and form a fundamental aspect of who we are as a person. For instance, someone with a strong spiritual belief in compassion may prioritize kindness and empathy in their interactions, making it a defining feature of their identity.

As we progress in life, visit new places, meet new people and have new experiences, our value system expands. We understand the same things from different perspectives. If the experiences are positive, they contribute to developing a value system that is 'inclusive'. If, on the other hand, the experiences are negative, this leads to cynicism and often to a value system or a point of view that is 'exclusive'.

It is a question of how you want to shape your value system to be—inclusive or exclusive. The more inclusive it is, the more resilient it will be in difficult times.

Education

Education is a very significant element of our identity, as it is usually directly related to what we do. For example, a technology professional will most probably have a technical education. What you studied, at which institution, and even what grades you had—all of this sometimes comes up in a discussion when we talk about ourselves.

If your education or degree happens to be from a premier

institute, it is often worn like a medal of honour, and every effort is made to make it conspicuous. It is only natural that we emphasize what we value and what we consider to be worldly recognition.

For those who have not had much luck with education, the lack of it sometimes constitutes their identity. When someone drops out and makes it big in life, it is often shared as a contrast to undermine the role of education in success. Many founders who are extremely successful today are not from IIMs or IITs, and when you talk to them or listen to them on podcasts, you often hear how they made it despite not coming from well-known colleges. Some of them even brag about being invited to the same college to speak to the students they had once failed.

Apart from the degrees and skills you acquire in education, the place of education influences, modifies and sometimes augments your beliefs and value system. You meet people from diverse backgrounds, mingle with them, learn about their social and economic conditions, and broaden your perspective. During my master's programme, I was among a group of students who came from different parts of Odisha, some from remote villages. Until then, my perspective was limited to meeting friends and students from my city. As I met and interacted with them, I was able to understand a whole new diversity around me. It also exposed me to various divides among students from different communities, regions, languages, etc. Sometimes it helps you build empathy; sometimes it makes your views (about the existing divide) so strong that you identify with a group. Education (and the environment in the institution) can also shape your political views and allegiances.

Education is a critical element of our identity, and it does play a significant role in how we evolve in life.

Hobbies and interests

Hobbies and interests are fascinating aspects of one's identity. As children, we are put into various subjects such as painting, music, sports, etc. We were probably into these until we found one that interested us and that we wanted to be good at. Nowadays, in many schools, especially the premium international ones, there are clubs such as painting clubs, music clubs and public-speaking clubs that students join during school hours. Most schools also organize competitions on these hobbies as part of extracurricular activities. Hobbies and interests are yet another tool of competition. Once we move into the more academically intensive classes, hobbies and interests go out the window, and the focus of parents and students returns to the race for grades and marks.

I know a well-to-do family with well-educated parents. Their daughter was interested in taking up tennis as a professional sport. She had talent, and she was putting in the hard work. Her parents seemed to be invested in her tennis career. They would also accompany her to various tournaments. When she was in ninth grade, she suddenly stopped taking tennis lessons and only focused on her studies. I later found out that after twelfth grade she had joined a very good engineering college. I'm not blaming anyone here. The problem is how we understand and perceive things from a decision-making perspective. The chances of the girl succeeding as a tennis player in India are less than the chances of getting a job. Admittedly, though, success in these two fields is widely different. The question is whether she should have continued having tennis as a hobby along with pursuing her engineering degree. Can hobbies and interests prevail over traditional career options?

After school, life gets busy with college, professional degrees and jobs. That 99 per cent of us give up our hobbies and interests is no exaggeration.

Very few people stay connected to their hobbies and interests. When you have a hobby, you feel a deep sense of connection when you pursue it. I am a painter, and when I paint, I feel completely connected to myself and disconnected from the worries and stresses of the world. I also see this as an opportunity to create something of my own. Painting is an integral part of my identity. My father has a great interest in books. He is an accomplished writer and reads a lot. Even after his retirement, he keeps himself busy in the world of literature. That is also part of his identity. I would like to leave you with a question to reflect upon: Which hobbies or interests are part of your identity?

Good citizen: Being responsible

We are all citizens of a country. That gives us identity. Is citizenship enough as an identity? Are we responsible, dutiful and law-abiding, or do we demonstrate selective adherence, through indulging in actions such as irresponsible driving, tax evasion, littering in public places and breaking cleanliness rules?

The paradox can be seen in many everyday scenarios. I have a friend who gets a kick out of changing lanes while driving. I don't understand how anyone can get pleasure out of this kind of driving. Not only is it uncomfortable to sit next to him, but it's also a problem for other drivers.

In an apartment society, there was this cleanliness drive where the residents were educated about how to dispose of garbage: how to separate dry and wet waste, how to segregate waste, how to discard medical waste, etc. All of us were educated (literate), but many residents simply dumped everything into one garbage bag, causing problems with disposal. Even after repeated reminders, people didn't stop, and ultimately it stopped when fines and penalties were imposed, with many disputing the quantum of the fines and penalties.

Many people in India evade taxes. For salaried folks, tax is deducted at source; hence, nothing much can be done, but some find creative ways like forging rent receipts to evade taxes. Businesses and the self-employed have more opportunities to evade taxes, which many do.

With growing internet usage, a new kind of problem is emerging in our civic sense. Recently, I was travelling on a train from Kolkata to Bhubaneswar. It was a chair car. After a long day of travelling, I had finally found my window seat, leaned back, and was about to drift into a well-earned nap when bam, the unmistakable sound of an Instagram Reel behind my seat jolted me back to reality. The passenger behind me had decided that the entire coach needed to hear an influencer's dance number to a Bollywood song at full volume. Irony at its finest.

Lately, I've noticed that public transport is turning into an open-air cinema, minus popcorn. People seem to think it's perfectly acceptable to watch videos or listen to music through loudspeakers as if the rest of us had signed up for a community listening experience. This does not just apply to adults, but also toddlers who are handed mobile phones blasting nursery rhymes loud enough to summon a Disney character in real life.

I'm all in favour of staying entertained when travelling, but a little courtesy cannot hurt. We all preach respect, empathy and kindness in our lives, so why not extend the same values to our daily interactions?

I have tried to express my concern to some people who indulge in this act. Only a few complied; some stared at me, and the rest even got back at me. I realized that most people simply accepted this as the new reality.

Without further argument (and prioritizing my mental peace), I put on my noise-cancelling headphones and blissfully drifted off to sleep. Some battles are simply not worth fighting.

Citizenship is not just about which country we belong to. It is also about how we behave and contribute to the whole idea, duty and responsibility of citizenship, and this is an integral part of one's identity.

Good Samaritan: Giving Back to Society

Most of us probably live a life in which we chase after some goal. We stay busy, work hard, and when we reach the goal, we revise the goal. This happens to many of us. A friend of mine used to grumble about his job, saying that he would quit if he reached a certain number of milestones. Every time I meet him, he gives me a revised number. Does that sound familiar? Can you relate to it? The fact is that we are so engrossed with our own goals that we rarely bother about others.

Yet there will be many of us who want to do something for others, to give something back to society, but don't know how to go about it. We are busy, and that makes it difficult to find a channel. Still, there are some good Samaritans who contribute to society, albeit in small ways. Here are two examples: one on a large scale and the other on a small scale, but each has a certain dimension.

In 2015, a 35-year-old lawyer from Mumbai, together with his 84-year-old neighbour, began cleaning up the garbage- and filth-filled Versova beach. Since that eventful year, a lot has happened, and Afroz Shah and his neighbour, the late Harbansh Mathur, are now known the world over. Afroz admitted to being an ocean lover and that looking out of the window and seeing heaps of garbage every day filled him with sorrow. He decided to change that. Following the words of Mahatma Gandhi, 'If you want to see a change, be the change yourself,' this man's journey began. Soon this clean-up drive assumed gigantic proportions, and people from all walks of life, including celebrities, big organizations, college students and municipality workers, joined hands. The clean-up drive had turned into a revolution. Afroz Shah gave his time to give back to society.

If we want to give back to society, there are numerous ways to do so. For example, you could work on a pro bono basis at the grassroots level in schools. You could help raise awareness about certain subjects, such as financial inclusion in villages and remote places. All of this will require money, but more than money, it will require your time.

Let's move on to example number two: your contribution doesn't need to be grand; it doesn't have to impact the environment or have to do with world peace. Even a little help can make a big difference. My friend regularly supports a family since the main breadwinner is unable to work. Likewise, there are numerous other examples where people have provided financial assistance to the needy. In this case, it's not my friend's time but his money. The effort may not be huge; it may be minuscule. However, imagine the impact on the family.

Whether you can give time or money is not the question. Nor does the scale matter. The question is whether you have the intention. If you have the intention, you will willingly find a way to do it. *When you are going through a rough patch yourself, take the time to help others. You will feel much better, much more fulfilled, and much greater than you originally felt.* There are many ways you can give back to society, and this is an aspect of your identity that you often overlook or completely ignore.

What is Identity?

Based on my friend's experience, my research and my views on identity, I have come up with various elements that could constitute our identity. These could be individual-specific, cohort-specific, and some generic ones. As I reflected on each of these elements, I realized that they are all part of identity in their own important way. So where does our interpretation of identity sometimes go wrong?

Imagine a plank balanced by multiple pillars. If one of these pillars is taken out, it will cause damage, but the chances of everything collapsing are less. Think about yourself and your pillars, and then you will truly know what your identity is. Invest time and energy in these elements that matter, and your life becomes more fulfilled. Your identity is something that cannot be taken away from you. The one who is aware of their identity is the one who has the most resilience and inner peace.

4

Decisions

'Sometimes you make the right decision; sometimes you make the decision right.'

—Phil McGraw

In the famous poem 'The Road Not Taken' by Robert Frost, the poet talks about choosing between two paths. As the poet looks ahead, he sees two roads diverge into the 'yellow wood'. And yes, he can't take both at the same time. He looks at both, and both have their way of tempting the poet to choose them. The poet chooses the road less travelled and makes a mental note of the other for another day, knowing fully well that he may not be able to return to undertake the journey. The poet decides and confesses that he had chosen the road less travelled, and that has made all the difference.

In life, we come across many crossroads where we must make decisions. Often the choices we must make are equally desirable or undesirable. When confronted with a choice, we find it easy to make decisions when there is a clear alignment of priorities. However, this is rarely the case. By and large, we encounter situations where making a choice between two or more equally desirable or undesirable decisions becomes inevitable.

We all make decisions. Some make them more often and more quickly, while many are slow and indecisive, and tend to procrastinate. Nevertheless, making decisions is part of everyone's lives, no matter how we go about it.

In psychology, decision-making is a cognitive process that leads to the selection of a particular course of action from several available alternatives.

A very rudimentary decision-making process would involve the following:

1. **Identifying the decision:** For example, choosing a university or a job.
2. **Gathering information:** Collect as much information as possible about the decision.
3. **Finding and evaluating alternatives:** Generate probable options and evaluate these options based on the information gathered.
4. **Choosing between the alternatives:** Pick the option that best suits your objective.
5. **Executing and monitoring:** Execute the decision and monitor the impact.

It is important to distinguish between problem-solving and decision-making. Problem-solving is sometimes used interchangeably with decision-making. However, there is a subtle difference. Problem-solving is the process of gathering information, processing information and developing alternatives that eventually lead to decision-making when one of the many recommended alternatives is considered.

What different factors might influence decision-making? Let's explore a few of them.

Fear of Making Decisions

Many of us suffer from the dilemma of whether decisions are good or bad. In my opinion, decisions are not good or bad; it is the consequences that are good or bad. We make the decision based on the best judgement we can make. In hindsight, things may not turn out as they should, and we feel that we have made a bad decision.

It is the fear of making a bad decision that causes the whole decision-making process to falter. As a result, people tend to make decisions that they perceive as 'safe' or 'socially recognized', and believe that everything will be ok. This approach prevents alternative viewpoints or choices from being recognized and accepted. Two good friends of mine studied together at school, and they were good students and scored well in the matriculation (tenth standard) exam. One of them never had a preference for science subjects, despite the socially recognized norm that good students in his town at the time opted for science subjects. He opted for the humanities. He did very well academically and joined India's most coveted service, the Indian Civil Service. Another friend, who also disliked the science stream, couldn't take that path and opted for science because he chose a 'safe' and 'socially recognizable' path. He didn't do well in science and yet pursued the subject in graduation too. Somewhere along the line, he lost his way and couldn't realize his potential. The point here is not to discuss how their careers unfolded or that one was better than the other. Instead, I would like to highlight a few things.

- Both made the decision based on what they thought was right for them.
- One of them was able to realize his potential, while the other lost his way.
- The fear of getting it wrong prevents many people from making the choices that they should make, as against the choices they actually make.
- The fear of getting it wrong is nothing more than the fear of failure.

Times have changed, and they are still changing. Today, people have become more self-aware. Failure is not really failure but part of the process and offers immense learning. Sometimes it is even celebrated. The more self-aware you become, the more information you gather, and the better you can decide what's good for you. Once you have decided, you must go all out and back your conviction. It's not the decision you make that will help you succeed. It's how you put your whole self behind the decision you make, the conviction behind your decision, that matters the most.

Stress of Decision-making

Each of us has experienced stress when faced with a choice. It is not the decision that causes stress; it's the tussle in the background that stresses us out before we make a decision.

A friend of mine was fed up with his current job and started looking for other opportunities. The market was booming, and his skills were in demand. Hence, it didn't take him long to land a job interview and an offer. This is where the story gets interesting. After he got the offer, he also applied to two other companies and was successful there too. Now he had three offers to choose from and was in almost 'three minds' about which one to accept. Choosing one meant he had to let go of the other two. This stressed him out as he was unsure which one to take. He reached out to many people to help him decide. Each point of view confused him and fuelled his anxiety. After much discussion and deliberation, he was finally able to make his decision. Once he had made his decision and informed the key stakeholders, he was satisfied. From the time of the dilemma to his decision, those were times of great anxiety and stress.

People tend to go around in circles and are unable to take a call. As a result, the stress keeps mounting, and suddenly the whole process of arriving at a decision seems unsolvable, and the decision is made automatically with time. Please avoid this vicious circle. Keep a cool mind, be rational, talk to people who can give you expert advice, and keep reminding yourself that you need to make a decision.

Financial Aspects of Decision-making

An extremely important aspect of decision-making is the money involved in it. In life, we are often faced with various choices, such as which house to buy, which school to send our children to, which hospital to opt for, where to go on holiday, and so on. In most of these decisions, the cost and financial implications play a major role. If finances were not a constraint, decision-making would be a cakewalk. Unfortunately, that is not the case. We all have our financial constraints, limitations, etc. Hence any decision-making framework has a financial component to it.

A boy from a wealthy family worked for a multinational software company. His father and mother were healthy and, like many other older people in their community, went for their morning walks, did yoga, etc. They also ate a relatively simple diet, and everything was going well. One night, the father complained of acute pain in the left side of his body. After a check-up in the hospital, doctors found that he had a severe arterial blockage and needed to be operated on and fitted with a stent. This was shocking news, as he was fit and healthy. His family now had to make the decision of choosing a hospital for his treatment. They chose one of the best hospitals in the city, and the whole procedure was a success. He also had health insurance, which pretty much covered all the expenses. Hence, it was just a matter of picking a hospital.

The second situation was that of another family that was not so wealthy. The son was in the last year of engineering college. When the father was diagnosed with a heart condition, it was not just the question of the hospital where the operation should be carried out, but also where it could be done at a reasonable price with good doctors. Since the best hospital would charge a fortune for such a procedure, they were quite stressed about where to get the money from. In the end, they sold a piece of land in their village and made arrangements for the financing, and the father was operated on. The operation was successful.

The two examples do prove a couple of things. Firstly, if you are not under financial constraints, most of the time the first set of decisions is usually easy for you. Secondly, when it comes to matters of life and death, you would look for the most optimal solution no matter what your financial constraints are. If you do not have the financial might, the search for the optimal solution will delay your decision-making.

Effective Decision-making

Information is the new power

For effective decision-making, you need access to information. Information helps you to understand the background and nature of the situation and consequently enables you to use your sense of judgement.

Friends and family

The first source of information is still friends and family. However, Google has made its way up there too, but more on that later. When we search for information, we usually ask our friends and family if they have any ideas or insights into the scenario. In most cases, you get a hint of the direction, and then you look for more information. However, most of the information may only be opinions. It is therefore necessary to verify the information and look for what is useful.

You may get some pointers from family, relatives and friends, but they may not be experts in the subject. In such a case, they are only clues, and you should broaden your search to gather more information.

Google to the rescue

As already mentioned, Google is the most frequently consulted expert these days. Even if we have the slightest doubt about something, we turn to Google for information. This is a very good thing, as it has helped many people move from opinions to facts. People share their real experiences, data and information over the internet, and nowadays there is a structured approach to this sharing of information. It is called 'content creation'. These days, it is almost a race between content creators for likes, shares and subscriptions, and honestly, I think this race benefits content consumers as more researched, quality content is shared across different platforms. With more and more content creators jumping on the bandwagon, content development is at its peak. While social media has made tremendous progress, I believe Google (along with YouTube) will most certainly be the first place to go when you are looking for information. Other social media aren't far behind either, but again, there is a specific case that we will discuss a little later.

At the time of writing this book, the top ten most frequently asked questions with their average monthly search volumes were:

What to watch?	9,140,000
Where's my refund?	7,480,000
How did you like that?	6,120,000
What is my IP address?	4,090,000
How many ounces in a cup?	2,740,000
What time is it?	1,830,000
How I met your mother.	1,830,000
Where am I?	1,500,000
How to lose weight fast.	1,500,000

Google classifies the questions in the 5W and 1H format (**W**hat, **W**ho, **W**hy, **W**here, **W**hen and **H**ow) so that people can access this information in their own ways.

The latest in this area is the advent of GenAI. Tools such as ChatGPT and Gemini have started to become the go-to tools for information, creativity and analysis. The speed at which GenAI has disrupted our lives is unprecedented.

Searching for information on Google or any other source is proactive, but what about the information being fed to us? Yes, I am talking about targeted advertising on social media.

Targeted advertisements

In the era of social media, most of us are active on various platforms. We create our profiles, share things about ourselves, celebrate our achievements, share our sorrows, and so on. This helps these platforms profile us very accurately. Technologies such as AI and ML are so accurate that it is no exaggeration to say that they know our needs better than we do. Many people express their deep privacy concerns, which is true to a large extent, but also imagine the positive side.

Let's say you want to try something specific and have no idea how to do it. You have tried the proactive way but still haven't made much progress. And suddenly you come across a social media advertisement that addresses exactly this pain point. Don't you think it raises your awareness with the information? Well, I think it does.

There are various other commonly known sources of information, such as newspapers, books and television channels. Nevertheless, the key message is that decision-making requires information availability and information processing. Without these, a decision will be more emotional than logical. However, we are human, and most of our decisions will be 'emo-logical'. For example, there is an ongoing debate about whether to buy a house or pay rent. No matter what the numbers look like, buying your first house satisfies a different aspect of your being. The decision is part emotional and part logical.

Past performance is not a guarantee of future performance

People tend to bring their experiences to the fore when making a choice. If you have had a bad experience with the outcome of a decision, you probably wouldn't immediately recommend that path for yourself if you found yourself in a similar situation again. Whereas if you had a great outcome, you are most likely to take the same path again. Past performance is no guarantee of future success. Things change over time. So, it is important to understand that applying the same decision in a similar situation over a period may or may not work. You need to suspend your judgement. Take your time, go through the information, remove your bias, and of course you can also draw on your experience. Every time you find yourself in a situation where you have to make a decision, you need to treat it like a fresh situation.

After I quit my job in 2021, I started my personalized mentoring programme. Until a few years ago, mentoring services, counselling and career workshops were sold offline, with the help of sales representatives calling prospective clients, making them understand the offer, and trying to get a financial commitment. Having worked in companies where I had sales teams that drove things the traditional way and were successful, I thought I would have to take the same route for the sales aspect of my mentoring programme, i.e., hire a sales team. I thought if I could prepare the offer deck, create a sales pitch, hire a couple of interns, train them, and ask them to make calls, it would all work out.

I was pretty sure that this was the right way forward, until I realized that the world had changed a lot in the meantime. Today, in the age of automation, such an old-school method will result in a poor return on investment (ROI), especially if the product or service is digital. I need to create automation around the sales and the funnel.

My current mentorship programme is completely automated. The only touchpoint is when clients feel and believe that the programme can help them, and they opt for a face-to-face video call. This method is less intrusive and, in many ways, puts discretion in the hands of the customer. As for me, it means I have an automated sales rep working for me 24 hours a day, and I don't have to bother about their sales skills, lead generation, etc. It's a win-win situation for everyone. This example demonstrates how past thinking can become a roadblock. You need to treat each situation differently, even if you had encountered a similar situation in the past.

Timelines: Things should be time-boxed

The timeframe for decision-making is very crucial. If you decide in good time, things will move forward. If you delay the decision, other parameters creep in, doubts sneak in, and you can't decide then.

When investing in your career, after gathering and processing information, you will arrive at what you want to do. Then you find a career coach who can help you with your career growth. So you explore further and find out that the coach has a premium price tag. You would not be able to make a decision on the spot and ask for more time. What happens when you take more time to answer? You tend to forget information and begin to question the ROI and value of your judgement. The more you delay, the more likely you are to lose information.

The 'forgetting curve', developed by German psychologist Hermann Ebbinghaus in the late 1800s, hypothesises the decline of memory retention with time. The forgetting curve indicates people tend to forget up to 50 per cent of new information within an hour of learning it and 70 per cent within 24 hours. At the end of a week, people tend to retain only about 25 per cent of what they have learnt. So if you don't set yourself a personal deadline to decide whether or not to go for the course or programme, the chances are high that you will not choose it, irrespective of the great benefits it might bring you. So, what to do to get out of this situation to move the needle? *Always set a time frame in which you have to make a decision.* It is either a yes or a no, but make the choice. Closure is more important than the outcome. Consciously break through your inertia. Keep moving.

Stakeholders—key to the outcome of the decision

An interesting part of decision-making is the question of who is affected by it. Suppose you want to quit your job; who else is affected? Your employer? No. Do not even entertain the thought that your absence will affect your employer in any way. You are very dispensable. Who is next then? Your family? Yes, very much. You may be the only breadwinner of the family, or you may not be financially dependent on them at all. So it is very important to understand the impact of your decision on the various stakeholders. A well-considered decision is always made taking into account the stakeholders. In 2021, I was working in an MNC and was based in Mumbai. Living and working in Mumbai was one of the best experiences of my life. There was no reason I could think of for moving out of Mumbai except to be with my parents in my hometown.

As you can see, there is a lot of 'I' in the above passage. But in reality, there was also a 'we'. My wife was equally fond of Mumbai, and she too had a job in this city. I didn't have the right to make this decision alone. We talked about it and together decided to move back to Bhubaneswar. While settling down was a challenge, we never had any conflict regarding the decision. We need to understand the role of the stakeholders in decision-making.

A similar decision didn't work out well for a family acquaintance who lived in the US and stayed there for a long time. During their stay in the US their children were born, and they were about twelve and ten years old when the family suddenly decided to move back to India. Once they were here, there were tremendous challenges for the boys to adjust to the new environment. It is fair to say that they were almost raised in the US—they were more American in many ways. The tussle continued for about a year, and finally one day the family packed up everything in India and went back to the US. Initially, when the father made the decision, he hoped that things would fall into place for the boys as they were still young. But that was not the case. Perhaps the key stakeholders were too young at the time of the decision to protect their interests or at least stand their ground. When not addressed, stakeholders can lead to very unfavourable outcomes.

Decisions are an integral part of our lives. They go beyond merely gathering information and making a choice—they run deeper. Sometimes, we must choose between two equally desirable or undesirable options. Fear can cloud our judgement. Past experiences can weigh heavily on us. Factors like money and time influence the process, and stakeholders add another layer of complexity.

But should this make decision-making overwhelming? No. Instead, we must recognize its complexity, understand its nuances, make informed decisions, and most importantly, back our convictions.

5

Hobbies and Interests

'The finest thing about a hobby is that you can't do any pretending about it. You either like it or you don't.'

—Dorothy Draper

A good friend of mine recently shared a painting on social media. It was a beautiful painting. I asked her when she painted it amid her busy schedule at the office. She said, 'Oh, that? That I painted when I was in school.'

Try to remember what things and activities we enjoyed as children. What did we do in our free time? Some of us liked to draw, some liked to sing, some played an instrument, many were into sports and extracurricular activities, and a few were all-rounders. As children, we had some kind of hobbies and interests that we were glued to for hours without needing anything to eat or drink.

As our student life progressed, these hobbies gave way to studies. While the number of classes went up, the actual importance of these hobbies in our daily lives went down.

The same hobbies we were once encouraged to pursue started taking a backseat and, in a few years completely faded from view for many of us.

Once we finished school, there was college and the pressure to do well, which would eventually lead to good earnings, a job and a livelihood. So hobbies and interests had no place in our grand scheme of things. Studies, coaching and preparations for big entrance exams sucked everything out of us, leaving us with little time, energy and interest for our hobbies.

Youthful exuberance and the zest to make a mark in our careers put us in a race, and we find ourselves in a situation where we are always in a hurry and never on time. In all of this, hobbies lie dormant in our lives, waiting for a call. For most, the call never comes, and only a very few find the call, albeit late.

In this day and age, our work takes up the lion's share of our time. For many of us, all we do after work is watch streaming services or browse social media, express our views on it, and then maybe have food and sleep. At the weekend, we probably watch a movie or visit a mall, and then the daily grind of another week begins. Life enters into a set sequence of events that are repeated week after week, month after month, and year after year.

But for some of us, the story is not the same. These people have managed to maintain their hobbies and interests right from the beginning. Do they do things differently? How do they achieve this amid the madness and perpetual grind? Can we learn something from such powerful stories of real people? Let's explore.

The Writer-IAS Officer

An IAS officer has a very dynamic career, from working in the field to dealing with pandemics, floods, endemic diseases, droughts and law and order. Stress and high pressure are synonymous with the jobs of IAS officers. Most of us only see the power and prestige of IAS officers, but behind this power and prestige is a strong sense of responsibility, commitment and a promise about public service delivery against the backdrop of a stressful and political environment. Under these circumstances, everyone is bound to be overworked.

My father is a retired IAS officer. He is also a very well-known writer in India, primarily contributing to Odia literature. My father is always calm and composed when faced with adverse situations. This always amazed me, and when I asked him what made him so calm, he replied that, among many other things, reading and writing (authorship) were critical anchors.

From childhood, he had a keen interest in reading and writing. Born in a village where the literary institutions were not worth mentioning, he would walk miles to read magazines, books and newspapers in the nearby town library. He slowly started developing an interest in writing and began to write articles, which were published in newspapers and magazines when he was still a student.

With time his reading and writing reached the next level, and he began to write books—prose, poetry, children's books, song lyrics and translations. He went on to establish himself as a leading author of Odia literature, winning many literary awards.

On the career front, he held many critical positions in the state administration, rising to the rank of chief secretary. Even after his retirement, he served the state government when he was appointed as chief election commissioner and later chairman of the finance commission. An exemplary and equally illustrious career as an administrator and a writer—only a few can dream of it.

The most common excuse for not pursuing a hobby is that we are busy, work long hours, and have to deal with work stress. This example perfectly illustrates how to achieve this balance—how to find time for the things that are close to your heart and give your life meaning.

So, if you know what makes you feel alive, find that thing and see how your life changes.

The Guitarist-IT Professional

In the early years of my career, I worked with an IT company. I met a person who worked with me in the same department but on a different project. To be honest, I never interacted with him, but I heard many interesting things about him. Most of the good things I had heard about him were related to his work. Besides all these things, I also heard a lot about his passion for playing the guitar. I learnt that he tried to play the guitar every day. When he was posted abroad to the UK, he carried his guitar with him. For the rest of us who had even a small talent for anything, a job life meant giving up that hobby in favour of relaxation. For him, playing the guitar was his relaxation. His passion gave him recognition outside of work. IT professionals are known for working long hours, especially when deadlines are just around the corner. He always found time, if not every day, to play the guitar and connect with his inner self.

As humans, we have varied interests, but most people don't have the awareness to commit to and stay engaged with their hobbies and interests. For many, their whole life goes by without them engaging in their dormant interests. Only a lucky few manage to set the wake-up call in motion. In my opinion, it's *'better late than never. I'm one of those late bloomers when it comes to hobbies.'*

Back to My Basics

For most of my career, I have had a corporate job. I started in tech companies, and after completing my MBA, I moved into management consulting and then into strategy roles in an industry with large conglomerates. While this career trajectory brought professional growth and financial stability, it also came with significant stress. Deadlines, targets, stakeholder management and the relentless pressure to perform often left me drained. Amid the intense focus and constant demands, there were moments when my work felt meaningless, as if it lacked any real impact.

The corporate world has a way of turning even the most exciting tasks into routine. The constant grind—home to job, job to home, and repeat—gradually wore me down. I realized that the more I was caught up in the daily hustle, the less room there was for creativity or personal growth. The pressure to deliver results left little time to think outside the box or pursue ideas that genuinely excited me. It was as if my creative instincts had been dulled by the monotony of work and the stress that came with it. In corporate machinery, efficiency often takes precedence over imagination, and that can make you feel like just another cog in the wheel. This realization prompted me to explore ways to reignite my creativity and find meaning beyond deadlines and deliverables. I wasn't sure what to do or how to get started.

I remember my father insisted on me engaging in a hobby to turn my stress into something creative. But as I mentioned earlier, in my quest to make my mark, I had completely disregarded his life-saving tip.

One day I saw one of my daughter's paintings, and it rekindled my childhood interest. I had a talent for painting, and I painted quite well at school, entered competitions and won many prizes (I am sure many of us have participated in Fevicryl contests and won medals). Growing up, the pressure of studies and jobs mounted, and I didn't touch the brush for a very long time, maybe twenty years or more.

So when I looked at one of her paintings, I just took

the brush and painted a little picture of hibiscus. Something changed in me that day, and I started painting again. What followed was an extremely intense phase of learning. I started learning from YouTube, bought courses and even took some live classes. Initially, I feared that my paintings wouldn't turn out well, and honestly, many times they didn't, and I came close to giving up. Soon it became more about expressing myself than anything else.

Painting became my relaxation time, my meditation time. Even in the busiest of times, I could find time to paint, even if it was only a little one. Much like the guitarist IT professional, finding time for my hobby became a habit.

I painted so much that the house was filled with them. The better I got, the more professional the paintings started looking. Then someone suggested that I could sell them or give them away as gifts.

Perhaps the biggest return I received from my hobby was that it gave me the ability to overcome the grief of losing my mother. I spent hours painting, and it slowly began to heal me and help me fill the void.

Being able to cultivate hobbies from childhood and somehow stay connected to them in adulthood is extremely rewarding in terms of attaining balance and well-being in life. To all parents: Please push your children to practise hobbies as much as you push them to study hard. You would be doing them a great favour and probably giving them the most invaluable gift of their lives.

How COVID-19 Changed Our Relationship with Hobbies

COVID-19 and its impacts were something the modern world had not seen before. Despite so many advancements in technology and medicine, it proved that we were all on our knees—powerful countries and people to poor countries and ordinary mortals—and we all had to surrender to the wrath of the deadly virus.

One thing COVID did was force us all into our homes, and so began the work-from-home regime. Working from home brought many challenges in the beginning, such as no fixed hours, and working from home meant constant availability. This led to mental health issues, but soon people were able to come to terms with the new normal and realized they had more free time at their disposal. That's when a lot of people revitalized their otherwise dormant hobbies.

The singer-professor

I am sure that most of us who like singing will relate to my next anecdote. As a child, I would write lyrics of Hindi movie songs that I wanted to sing. I always wanted to sing to music, and the only opportunity to do so was at the school annual functions. Children who took part in the celebrations mostly sang devotional or patriotic songs. However, I was a big fan of Hindi film songs. The desire to sing to music stayed with me. It was only much later in life that I learnt about karaoke.

Nowadays there are apps such as StarMaker and Smule that offer the opportunity to do karaoke, thus fulfilling the wishes of many like me who had long forgotten about singing.

A professor at an MBA college who had an innate talent for singing but was not a trained professional began singing with the help of StarMaker as COVID gave her that extra time to dabble in her interest.

It was great fun to have fulfilled a childhood wish—singing along with the music. The more she sang, the more she came into contact with people who were also on the same singing platform. What began as an interest turned into a full-blown passion. Today, she takes part in contests, records her music videos for YouTube, participates in events, and most importantly, she has become part of a community of like-minded people and has expanded her network immensely. She was invested in this endeavour not for fame or glory but for self-expression and a sense of fulfilment.

In the post-COVID era, many people turned to their hobbies to feel connected and rejuvenated. In many ways, it has helped them to rediscover who they are and also inspire many others.

The question is: when is the best time to develop a hobby? Well, childhood is the most favourable time to develop a hobby. Develop it and get better at it so that you can enjoy it most in your youth, middle age and old age.

But if for some reason you have your hobby locked up in your heart and won't let it get out, any time is a good time to do so. Make that wake-up call.

For people who missed the bus, you can still develop hobbies at a later time in life. There is a challenge in starting late that one must be aware of. Because hobbies, like any other thing in life, take time before they start to become fun. If people don't see progress, they quit. If you want to play the guitar, for example, you need a lot of practice and time until you can play something meaningful. So many people give up when practising is boring and progress is slow. You have to keep at it and trust the process. Soon you will see progress, and then there will be no stopping you as you learn and have fun.

The next question is: How do you choose your hobby? The answer is: it depends. However, let me give you a few pointers. Start by taking an interest in something you loved as a child. Start engaging with it. Give it time and then see if it works for you. The best part is, if you don't like it or don't enjoy it as much as you thought you would, you can always do something else. No one is judging you, and you don't judge yourself. That's the best thing about hobbies. I had a friend who was interested in modern dance. He hired a teacher and started taking lessons. Soon he realized he had no talent for it and enjoyed watching more than doing it himself. He is still figuring out what his NEXT is.

Despite all the bliss and satisfaction, can hobbies be a serious career option?

Hobbies as Career Moves

A proverb generally attributed to the great Chinese philosopher Confucius reads, 'Choose a job you love, and you will never have to work a day in your life.'

Although there is much truth in this adage, for many people this idea remains out of reach, as there are many factors that determine how we earn money in life.

Often hobbies are not seen as profitable and may not generate enough money for livelihood or the kind of life and lifestyle we want. This is one of the main reasons why people force themselves into traditional jobs because they pay better and offer stability. However, some bravehearts among us take the plunge and choose a profession, job or freelancing work that is connected to their hobbies and interests. Let's explore a few of these inspirational stories.

The Zumba-IT professional

In one of the IT companies that I worked in, there was a girl who was quite a fitness freak. At a time when we wanted to party hard with our well-earned money from our first jobs after college, she was busy sweating it out at the gym.

She tried to talk us into health and fitness, but in the arrogance of youth, many of us made fun of her for depriving herself of the good things in life, such as great food (read junk) and late parties. She was, however, determined, and apart from the occasional cheat day, she was always focused.

Over time, I changed companies, moved houses, and lost contact with her. I'm sure she moved places too and was doing well. One day, I saw a social media advert where she was promoting her Zumba classes. I checked her Instagram profile and realized that she was a fitness influencer with a huge following. She creates health- and fitness-related content.

She endorses gyms, health and fitness products, and earns a commission from them. Through mutual contact, I learnt that she had quit her job and was doing this full-time. Offering Zumba classes was a natural extension. That she had chosen this field was no surprise, but the 'altering arc' she had taken inspired me greatly.

The astrologer-business analyst

My college friend had an interest in astrology and palmistry. In college, he was extremely popular for this, and I know of numerous occasions when he took advantage of this. In the first year, when we were going through 'formatting' (read: ragging), he was the only one the seniors singled out and asked for astrological readings. Well, the seniors were approaching job placement season and were naturally scared and wishing for divine intervention. These seniors ended up shielding my friend on many occasions.

College got over, and we went into our respective jobs. He joined a company and worked as a business analyst and did well. While work kept him busy, he studied astrology formally, taking courses and gaining certifications. He soon realized that people were dissatisfied with their careers and wanted a promotion, a salary hike, or a job change, and here too, the desire for divine intervention was very strong. He recognized the gap and specialized in astrology, intending to help people with their careers. He has put in a lot of hard work alongside his regular job; and today, as we speak, he is all set to quit his job and take up astrology as a full-time profession.

Perhaps one of the greatest things that hobbies and interests do is contribute to shaping one's identity. People with well-developed hobbies and interests tend to have stronger resilience when it comes to their identity. This helps them to cope better with adversity and lead an engaged and fulfilling life.

6

Seeking Help

'Be strong enough to stand alone, smart enough to know when you need help, and brave enough to ask for it.'

—Anonymous

A heart-touching video that did rounds on social media showed a man with two cigarette lighters. He put one of the lighters into an empty jar and began to pour out water little by little. Each time he poured out water, the video mentioned an adversity in life, such as the loss of a loved one, the loss of a job, a financial crisis, and so on. And at the end, he takes the lighter out of the jar and lights it. Obviously it doesn't light. *The lighter had lost its spark.* The second lighter, on the other hand, worked perfectly. *It was able to produce a spark inside.* Then came the moment of truth: The man took the second lighter and lit the first one (the wet one) with it, and lo and behold, the first lighter also got the spark back.

When people go through difficult times, they are unable to awaken their inner spark. Sometimes all you need is a little helping hand.

The only question is where this helping hand should come from.

When the chips are down, you tend to seek help from your immediate family, relatives and friends. These people are the first circle of help we reach out to. When we approach our inner circle for help, we usually have expectations. We have expectations because we know these people, and they know us. We expect that the helping hand will simply lift us out of the difficult situation. But when that doesn't happen, we are disappointed.

If you don't get help easily and your struggle seems to continue with no clear signs of improvement, please understand that there is a message here: *God wants you to walk the path alone. God wants you to find a way to get help and support to build your own path.* Remember the adage: God helps those who help themselves.

If you change your outlook and think about how you can prepare yourself to ask for help beyond your inner circle, you will see how instead of feeling disheartened about not getting help, you now focus on efforts to help yourself.

How do we bring about this change in mindset? Here are some steps that I have found useful about *how to get yourself to help yourself.*

How to Get Yourself to Help Yourself

Helping yourself is one of the hardest things to do, especially when going through a difficult time in life. When we are in a soup, pessimism engulfs everything we think and do. We visualize the possibility of failure more and give our efforts to succeed less chance. Everything thrown at us as a suggestion or recommendation seems like a Herculean task to get started with. No matter what we try and do, things don't seem to move, and we completely turn a blind eye to our efforts or lack thereof. This feeling is true for everyone.

I run workshops and training courses in corporates and colleges. In the early days of reaching out to colleges for conducting workshops, I didn't get enough response from them. This led me to form a pessimistic view that colleges would not respond to me. One day, a friend came over to my house, and when I shared my pessimistic outlook, he asked me point-blank about how many colleges I had reached out to. On reflection, I realized that the number of colleges I had reached out to was too small to conclude anything, but was it my tendency towards pessimism at the time that led me to arrive at this conclusion? I immediately changed my approach, worked on a better pitch, and started reaching out again. And to tell you the truth, after trying relentlessly, I got some wonderful responses. So, can we put a structure around *how to get yourself to help yourself*? Let me give it a shot.

Here are the four steps to do this.

1. **Accept you need help:** Many of us know that we are in

trouble or that we are in a difficult situation. We know that we need to get out of this situation, but we are simply not prepared to make the effort. There are various reasons why we stop ourselves from seeking.

Ego is perhaps the most common reason. Many people believe that they can do everything on their own and that no one else can teach them a thing or two. It is this ego that comes in the way of accepting help because it prevents them from understanding what is important. In my mentorship programme, I had a mentee who narrated an incident he had experienced. When he enrolled in my programme, he didn't tell a whole lot of people, and only a handful of his closest friends knew about it. But somehow a few people found out and the first comment he got from them was why he couldn't do it himself. *You don't need anyone to tell you. Are you so bad that you need help?*

The problem is how these people view 'help'. They see mentorship as a kind of supervisor-subordinate relationship where a supervisor has a dominant position. By becoming a mentee, you put yourself at the mercy of another supervisor outside of work. In reality, mentorship is not like that. It is anything but a relationship between supervisor and subordinate. Every great player in the history of any sport has had coaches and mentors. Roger Federer, considered one of the greatest of all time, had a coach. What on earth can a coach teach the best player in the world? And yet he had a coach. Did that make Roger inferior? Not at all. In fact, all players have coaches. Only people who can put their ego aside can see this aspect of mentorship.

The second most common reason is that *we focus so much on the problem that it becomes huge and seems unsolvable*. The famous Dwayne Johnson (The Rock) once said, *'When you focus on you, you grow. When you focus on the shit, the shit grows.'* I met with a fellow corporate professional at a conclave where we both were invited to speak. During our conversation, this gentleman started talking about his problems at work, and he kept going on and on. I was quite surprised, because we hardly knew each other before this conclave, and yet he was talking to a stranger about his issues. Nevertheless, the point is that the gentleman was so bothered by the problem that he hardly said anything about how it could be solved. For him, the problem was unsolvable, even with a change of job.

The third reason I want to talk about is that *we know the problem and the solution, but we just can't be bothered to take even the first step*. This is the classic case of expecting a silver bullet to come to the rescue. You wait and wait, rotting in a rut, and nothing seems to change. A close friend who wasn't happy at work kept switching jobs. After a few days or months in the new job, he found a problem that made him unhappy again.

He understood that changing jobs was not the solution. He knew that in order to be happy he would need help changing his outlook on life, and he should not base his identity solely on his job. Yet, he wasn't ready to move an inch in that direction. Maybe he needed a mentor. But he won't admit it, nor could he be bothered to find one. Sometimes you just get the feeling that he doesn't want to live an engaging and fulfilling life.

Last but not least, *we always look for quick fixes and free advice.* People like things for free. They want miracles to happen but are not willing to pay for them (effort or money). The stock market is booming, and the awareness of investing in stocks is way more pronounced than it was, say, ten years ago. It is common knowledge that many of us invest in stocks based on tips from friends and newspapers. How many of us subscribe to a stock recommendation service and pay a subscription for it? How many of us are willing to pay for a financial planning service? The fact is that people like quick fixes and are generally not willing to pay for expertise.

I once conducted a webinar on resume writing and had priced it at ₹99. I promoted the workshop through Instagram ads. After seeing the ad, a certain person wrote to me asking for a waiver on the grounds that he had lost his job. Do you think ₹99 is too high a price to pay if it directly helps your job search? Is it possible that the person is not spending any money anywhere else? Then why did he ask for a waiver?

The first step in dealing with problems is to accept that we need help. There is a price to pay in terms of effort and money (fees, etc.). No one is made worse off in life by seeking help. It is about moving on and getting out of the ditch, and if there is a price to pay, be prepared to pay it—see it as an investment.

2. **Expose yourself to serendipity:** The first step is to accept that you need help. The next step, of course, is to find out what kind of help you need. Sometimes we don't realize what kind of help we are looking for. One entrepreneur I know thought he needed help with digital marketing for his product, but the problem he needed help with was developing the right delivery models. Hence, it is important to find out what help is needed. On a personal level, it is even more difficult because you are the subject and are going through a tough time. Hence, it is difficult to find out straight away what help you need.

    A friend was stuck at work and was looking for a distraction or a hobby to take his mind off things. He had no idea what his hobby might be. His first step was to try things he had never explored before. He tried webinars on random topics to see what piqued his interest. He attended webinars on pranic healing, mental wellness, video editing, scriptwriting, diet and nutrition, public speaking, etc. What did this serendipity do for him? It helped him broaden his perspective. He experienced newer things in life. Trying different things helped him zero in on a few interests that could potentially become hobbies or a side hustle.

3. **Do not shy away from paid help:** Once you have worked out what help you need, it is now time to find out who can help you. As mentioned earlier, when you reach out

to your inner circle, i.e., your relatives and friends, you may or may not get any help. Typically, when we look for a job, the first thing we usually do is send our resumes to all our friends in other companies. Many of them upload it to the company networks, but you don't seem to get a call. It looks like the person didn't help you, but in reality they tried. A very important aspect to remember is that in your testing times, there will be many people who will try to help but may not be able to get an outcome. And there will be many who won't help. There is no way to differentiate. So just focus more on your goal, don't harbour a grudge, and move on.

Many of us tend to want things for free, and those that can help us with a quick fix. For example, when we want to change jobs, we ask someone approachable and with resume skills to take a look at our resume and give us free feedback. We then expect to be shortlisted and find a job. It's not just jobs; we don't want to pay for many things, especially not for advice.

However, any professional help or a long-term fix requires investment. Either you give time and learn, or you give money and have it done for you. For example, you can spend a lot of time and energy and understand the basics of financial planning, or you can hire a financial planner for a fee and help yourself get it done. The choice is yours, and you need to understand the trade-offs. If you do it yourself, you will need a lot of time, and you won't be sure if you are going in the right direction. With an expert, the time is reduced, and you can focus on other important aspects of the same solution.

Think of yourself as a company or an organization. When organizations need to get certain tasks done, they hire suppliers, consultants or contract workers, but they never want things done for free. Take the same approach. If you are sure that a particular paid help is right for you, don't shy away from it. Always look at the value it will bring, not the price you pay.

When deciding to opt for paid help in some shape or form, it is important to understand the various aspects involved in such a decision. The three important aspects of getting paid help include trust, transparency and price.

Use services or pay for services that you feel are in line with the outcome you are seeking and that you can live with. This is easier said than done. It is always going to be a trade-off. But please understand that price is the only aspect that is negotiable. Don't negotiate on the other two factors, even if the outcome looks alluring.

If you are looking for help and willing to invest, you will have to search, and you will probably burn your hands a few times before you find what is right and relevant for you. If you lose money in the process, don't be disheartened; don't lose faith. Trust the process. You will learn a lot.

The key takeaway is that you have to be *willing to accept help from anywhere and to invest time and money. You will see that this mindset will open more doors for you, even the ones that you had no clue about.*

4. **Be patient and work on your plan:** When we get help, we may not see results immediately. I'm talking about long-term solutions here, not short-term fixes. If you commit to a long-term process, results will be slow in the beginning. Over time, there is a cumulative and compounding effect, and at a certain point, the results are exponential. A high degree of patience is required to reach this stage. Again, easier said than done, so keep reminding yourself to stay calm.

If you can internalize this small framework, it will open up possibilities like never before. You will see yourself experimenting and trying new things, which will ultimately get you where you want to be.

I've been talking about getting help, but what about helping others?

Which Lighter Are You?

We must understand our role and responsibility with regard to helping others. Remember the lighter I talked about at the beginning of the chapter. While most of us would identify with the first one (the one that needs the spark), how many of us would step up and raise our hand to be the second one in someone else's life?

My experiences and observations during COVID-19 have shown me the importance of help. While it is said that COVID has made us value life more, and this is true too, being confined to our homes, working from home and literally living in silos have also made us a bit more self-centred than before. The need for each of us to help each other is greater now than ever before. Things have changed, and people have gone back to the old normal. If we have lost compassion, feeling for others, now is the time to get it back.

Be gentle; be kind. Sometimes all that the person in front of you needs is a hug and patient listening to rekindle the spark. There are numerous ways to help if you have the intention to do so. Just find ways to be the second lighter.

7

Giving Back to Society

*'It is not how much we give,
but how much love we put into giving.'*

—Mother Teresa

Many of us harbour the desire to give something back to society but end up doing little or nothing. There can be a plethora of reasons for this. Let me try to enumerate a few.

- Most of us are so busy organizing our lives that we do not have time to think beyond that. We practically slog during the week, and by the weekend we are too drained to do any good.
- Many older people who have time think that they can contribute via seminars and workshops, which, frankly, is not very effective. They also want to relax after working hard and primarily see these as 'engagements' to keep themselves busy rather than a means of impact.

- Some of us want to help, but we do not know how. So much so that we can't even bring ourselves to contribute to the old clothes donation drive in the neighbourhood.
- In such a state, giving back to society remains in the charitable hands of a few people or entities such as social workers and NGOs.

How can an ordinary person who has a desire to contribute do so?

Crowdfunding Platforms

In the good old days, when someone fell ill and needed money, the family usually turned to their friends and relatives, who willingly or reluctantly helped. Finding time amid a medical situation to reach out to people who could help was a task in itself. In the end, coming up with all the money required remained a very difficult task. Enter the crowdfunding platforms of modern times.

Crowdfunding platforms raise funds for a specific cause, which is usually medical in nature but is not limited to this. They have a funding goal that is required for the cause, and people donate to the cause. This is how the goal is achieved. The platform doesn't necessarily charge money for listing a cause and generally (at least that's what they claim) doesn't take money for listing services. However, if you want to run campaigns and advertisements, they do charge for these. Crowdfunding platforms are a great way to raise money.

- The one in need gets the money.
- The donor has a sense of giving back to society.
- And the platform plays a role.

All in all, it's a win-win situation for everyone.

In a short period, though, the online space has filled up with such online crowdfunding platforms. Many of them do not even verify the authenticity of the cause. A peculiar case of fundraising made the news when a young girl was trying to raise money on multiple platforms to study abroad. And what's more, people donated too. These platforms faced severe backlash from internet users. Studying abroad is a luxury, not a need. Cases like these call into question the authenticity of these fundraising campaigns.

While crowdfunding platforms offer busy people a great way to give back to society, at least with money if not time, it is important that people donate to the cause they identify with or want to support. They should do their own due diligence before making any financial commitment. It's not enough to donate; it's important that the cause is right and has a purpose.

NGOs conduct various kinds of drives in the locality such as donating of old clothes, toys, shoes, etc. This is an interesting way to contribute to society without it requiring too much time, money and energy. While people come forward to participate, many don't, citing reasons like laziness about getting up on a holiday, whether or not to trust the organization conducting the drive (especially around safety and hygiene concerns in blood donation camps), and so on.

Organizing for a Cause

There are very few among us who can put a cause above themselves. I talked about Mr Afroz Shah, who single-handedly took up the challenge of cleaning Mumbai's Versova beach. He is a celebrity social worker now.

What happened on my college WhatsApp group recently can serve as an example. A student of the current batch who was very ill was admitted to a private hospital in Delhi. His friends had started a crowdfunding campaign. While crowdfunding was progressing on its own, a professor in the group had taken it upon himself to raise awareness about the need for funds and convince people to donate. He himself donated a generous amount, and the best part was that the professor was not a relative of the patient. He took a personal interest in the case; he reached out to the family, comforted them, and shared the status of the family's well-being with us in the group. Isn't that just simply amazing? His service-above-self attitude is exemplary. It is people like him who make us believe that there is still hope for humanity.

Help with Money If You Can't Help with Time

Most of us are busy with our daily work, so it's difficult to find time to give to a cause. If you don't have time, you can donate money (of course, only if you are convinced and want to help). If you are open to this proposition, you will come across many opportunities, and it will be heartening to see how your humble contribution goes a long way. India is a large country with a diverse climate. There are enough natural calamities such as floods, droughts and earthquakes, etc. In such times, the government appeals to its citizens to donate generously. Look for such opportunities and donate and do your part in nation-building.

Try to Make it a Habit to Help Others

Helping is a state of mind. It is a noble intention that must be nourished again and again. The world is big, and there will be many opportunities to help. Just be on the lookout and inculcate a habit of helping others. The monsoon in Mumbai is beautiful. Many Mumbaikars look forward to the rain. However, it is also the most inconvenient time for commuters. One monsoon season in Mumbai, I was travelling with my family in an Uber (Chevrolet Beat). The road was slightly dug up, and there was a small pile of bricks in the centre of the road. Our car got stuck with the pile of bricks underneath it. We got out, and the driver and I wanted to push the car, but it was completely jammed. Just as we were thinking about what to do, an auto-rickshaw driver and two motorcyclists got out of their vehicles, and together the five of us literally lifted the car and cleared the bricks below it. As soon as the work was done, they all got into their vehicles and drove away without giving us a chance to thank them properly. If you have spent some time in Mumbai, you will know that I am talking about the spirit of Mumbai, which is to move on and help as we move.

I once visited a doctor in the Matunga area in south Mumbai. It was monsoon, and roads were waterlogged. There was a traffic jam, and vehicles were stuck. Fortunately, it stopped raining after some time, and the water started receding. Soon cars, bikes, buses and taxis came back to life, and there were traffic jams everywhere. The cops tried to clear the roads, but the jam had reached chaotic proportions. Suddenly I saw a few senior residents (maybe past their 60s) volunteering to clear the traffic jam. This is a scene I have seen so many times in Mumbai—the selfless help in times of need.

However, helping is not our second nature. In another city, I had parked my car (in the correct place). By the time I came back, I saw a few bikes and cars parked the wrong way around my vehicle. I looked around but couldn't find anyone, and after waiting for ten minutes with no sign of the owners, I decided to get the vehicle out by putting into use my (expert) driving skills.

I drove forwards, backwards, left and right, repeating the process, and it took me a while to get the vehicle out. As I wrestled with the car, I noticed two young people sitting in front of a tea stall sipping tea and constantly watching me (probably admiring my driving skills) and my efforts to manoeuvre the car. Maybe they were too busy doing nothing. Instead of coming to help me, they sat glued to the ground, discussing navigation strategies amongst themselves (which was evident from their hand gestures). After a few minutes, I managed to take out my vehicle (I really do seem to have expert-level driving skills).

The point is that helping people is a habit and an intention that not everyone has. If you are someone who at least has the awareness and the intent, make a conscious effort to develop this sense of selfless help.

Taking Giving-Back-to-Society to Next Level

My friend applied to renew his passport. He went to the passport office. Now that the process is streamlined, he was expecting no obstacles. The next step was the police verification. The day of verification came, and he went to his assigned police station. The official was quite overwhelmed with the immense workload. In addition to his normal duties, he also had the additional task of checking passport documents. Yet he went about his work silently and calmly. During this time at the police station, my friend realized that documentation work is tedious and that the police station was understaffed. Furthermore, police officers were also deployed for additional duties such as political functions, festival alerts, etc. In short, there was a twin problem: understaffing and multiple work allocations.

After waiting for the required time, when my friend's turn came, his documents were verified, and his job was done. Just as he got up, a thought occurred to him. He asked the police constable if he could volunteer to help with the document verification work on Saturdays. The police constable was surprised, as he had never been offered this kind of help before. He smiled and thanked my friend but said that this was not possible as they were handling personal documents, and therefore these could not be shared with an unauthorized person. My friend couldn't help, but it did drive home an important point: If you are willing to help, you will find ways to help. Some will work, some may not, but the idea is worth exploring.

Social Responsibility: Another Dimension of Giving Back

Giving something back to society doesn't always mean serving the community or helping people selflessly. There is also a completely different dimension. It is about doing your duty as a responsible social being.

- Spare a thought when you park your vehicle. Take time to understand that if you park anywhere, how inconvenient it could be for others. Some people just arrive and park. Everyone else may take a walk.
- India is a populous country. We must show restraint and observe discipline. Respect the queue. Develop some basic queue sense. A lot of people have this peculiar habit of standing right next to you rather than behind you. They wait, but it's just that their habit of standing close is annoying and intimidating.
- Avail yourself of what you subscribed to. Once I went to watch a movie. The movie had been playing for some time, so the theatre was quite empty. A family of three entered—husband, wife and child. Looking

at the empty seats, they just went to use the recliners although they had bought the standard tickets. The child protested that they should not sit on the recliners, as those were not their seats. However, the father and mother had decided to teach him the wrong lesson that day. They said that since no one was around, they could take those seats. The funniest part came after some time: the real seat holders came and they had to vacate. But do you know what they did? They just slid two recliners further but continued to use the recliners.

The idea is to be considerate of others when in public. Let us be mindful of others' convenience and leave our own self-centred worlds.

Giving back to society is a critical theme of life. Many of us are aware of it; some are actively pursuing it, but most don't know how to go about it. It is ultimately up to each of us how we want to deal with this life theme.

8

Relationship with Career

'Start by doing what is necessary, then what is possible, and suddenly you are doing the impossible.'

—Francis of Assisi

COVID-19 has changed the world forever. As the pandemic spread, the horrific sight of people dying and the countless families helplessly at the mercy of the pandemic completely transformed almost every aspect of human life. Naturally, the most common sector, 'work', couldn't have stayed inert during this unfortunate period in human history.

In the post-COVID era, our relationship with our careers is also changing. No one can say with certainty how it will evolve in the times to come.

COVID-19 had us in lockdown. Employees couldn't be called into the offices, and there was a feeling that work would stop. The knowledge-based companies that worked mainly with laptops and computers were the first to have business continuity. Core industries and sectors with plants and machinery were laggards in digitization and were clueless about what was next. The nation had gone into lockdown mode to break the cycle of the coronavirus, and most of us believed that after the lockdown period, things would be back to normal. Things didn't turn out as expected. There was no sign of the virus abating. Instead, it came back with a vengeance. No matter what we tried, lockdowns, shutdowns, or even *Holika dahan* of 'corona monster', nothing seemed to have any impact on this unprecedented catastrophe the world was facing. The catastrophe was such that it literally brought down powerful countries such as the US, China and India to their knees.

While all of this was happening, companies were grappling with the question of how to get their employees to work in the new scenario, as it was clear to everyone that COVID was not going away any time soon. As they say, necessity is the mother of invention; COVID forced even the most conservative employers to enable work from home. Suddenly, the demand for internet soared, and thanks to the infrastructure built by the telecom companies in India, the demand was suitably met. At that time, I happened to be working in a telecom company and was involved in initiatives related to enabling work from home for many organizations. Honestly, I felt like I was making my contribution to the nation and to the crisis, even though I was neither a doctor nor a police officer, whose contribution to society and humanity at that time cannot be described in words.

With the knowledge-based companies enabling work from home and other companies following suit, the era of work from home began in a form and manner that no one in their right mind could have ever imagined.

'Work from home' was an interesting era. Let me try to characterize this era with my interpretation. When this period began, many people, especially those living in big cities, were happy, as it meant no long and torturous commutes to the workplace. Commuting to offices is worse in the rainy season, as most big cities suffer from waterlogging. I was in Mumbai at that time, and everyone knows about the infamous Mumbai rains. Imagine not having to travel to office in the rain—a big relief. Everyone was more than happy to find this work-from-home job, and for starters, it saved the long and arduous journey to the office.

But life has a way of getting back. Although not having to commute was a blessing, the working-from-home arrangement soon turned into a nightmare. Firstly, not everyone's house was equipped with infrastructure, such as a dedicated working space with an ergonomic desk and chair, strong internet connectivity, etc. Parents with young children and toddlers at home used to have specific arrangements that allowed them to come to the office and dedicate time to work. With both parents working from home and alternative options like daycare not available, toddlers and kids spent the entire day engaged in activities inside the home during working hours.

Secondly, the physical start-stop that was the essence of a physical workplace ceased. Everyone in the workplace worked from home: managers, bosses, peers, cross-functional teams, etc. This meant that everyone was available at all times.

People were overworked and burnt out, and soon the focus was around mental well-being. Many organizations introduced mental wellness programmes, created virtual events for their employees, and ensured that the employees felt comfortable embracing work-from-home.

In the meantime, COVID was in full fury. Nobody could have imagined that the deadly disease would spread in wave after wave. The pandemic was wreaking havoc. As a result, working from home seemed to be the new reality, and employees and employers started accepting this new normal. Some companies carried out mass layoffs, especially those who were unable to work profitably.

Interestingly, working from home made people realize the priorities of work and life. They became more cognizant of their own life needs and understood that work was a part of life and not the whole of life. For many, free time and flexibility gave them an opportunity to rekindle hobbies and interests. Some used this time to create additional income streams for themselves.

Consequently, several workplace and career themes started trending. Some of the key trends worth mentioning are the Great Resignation, quiet quitting and moonlighting.

The Great Resignation

COVID-19 forced everyone to work from home. Even those who were laid off had no choice but to stay at home. Staying at home was distracting because the age-old idea of the 'office' is central to the working theme. People quickly adjusted and had time for family bonding, relationships, duties and responsibilities. While the job was earlier the sacrosanct dictator of our lives, it ensured that we did the minimum and outsourced most of what we might even like to take responsibility for. This newfound meaning of work, where the latter revolved around life's priorities and not the other way round, gave rise to a phenomenon called the 'Great Resignation'.

India was not far behind. In India, attrition mainly occurs in the tech sector, and earlier this attrition was primarily due to jobs with higher compensation. While there are numerous theories and hypotheses, the most common reason for this wave is work–life balance.

An interesting survey of people leaving their jobs and their expectations of their new jobs revealed some insights that were not entirely surprising.

Here are the most common responses:

- Forty per cent of the respondents cited burnout as the key factor.
- Twenty per cent cited a lack of flexibility at the workplace.
- Sixteen per cent felt that their current employer did not offer the right well-being programme.

When asked what they expected from their next job, if they wanted a new job at all, the responses were primarily centred on flexibility, remote working, and shorter workdays and weeks. Life should take centre stage, and work should adapt to it, not the other way around.

Quitting and finding something that matches your priorities is a bold move. People struggle to find the right balance. It is also possible that those who quit may, after exploring some options, simply want to return to their former 'working life'. There will be people and media who might just dub it as the 'Great Regret' after the 'Great Resignation'. These may not be prevalent today, but I see more and more people prioritizing their personal lives over their jobs and quitting even today. People now are seeking more meaning in their work. This is perhaps the new relationship with our work.

Quiet Quitting

While quiet quitting has nothing to do with actual quitting, it reflects a mindset where an employee is quite happy to 'meet expectations' and does not feel any need to go 'above and beyond'.

It all started when American TikToker Zaid Leppelin posted a video with the statement, 'Work is not your life'. Employees who quiet quit choose not to go above and beyond their work, including refusing to answer emails in the evenings or at weekends, or by skipping extra assignments outside of their core duties.

Here is why people took on the quiet quitting trend:

- This is a trend that is more apparent among Gen Z, who do not see the value of hustle in relation

- to reward and prefer a balance.
- The pandemic seems to have impacted the thought process such that many people now desire a work-life balance instead of the popular hustle culture.
- Many people do not see jobs as fulfilling the core of their life. They want to explore more.

While this is gaining momentum, not everyone seems to be on board. Counterarguments include:

- Doing the minimum or just meeting expectations means one must be content with mediocrity and hence will not accomplish anything significant.
- Salary increases and promotions are only given to those who go above and beyond, even if the increment remains at the same level.
- Quiet quitting is not the right attitude to bring to the workplace.

In my opinion, quiet quitting is not the right mindset to have. It is difficult to focus and deliver even the bare minimum when you are mentally checked out. I am not in favour of hustle either. In the changing world, finding a balance that works for you is the key.

Moonlighting

One benefit of working from home that people recognized was that the time freed up by not commuting could be used to turn a passion or side hustle into a source of income.

Although moonlighting refers to holding multiple jobs, I want to extend the definition to include side hustle where you work independently and offer your product or service (selling paintings, giving guest lectures, etc.).

Companies are now bringing the workforce back into the office; moonlighting or having a side hustle is going to be different. Nevertheless, having a side hustle or moonlighting is quite common these days.

The arguments in favour of moonlighting include:

- Once the employee gives their share of the time to the office and delivers the outcomes, the rest of the time belongs to them.
- In a constantly changing and volatile economy, a job can no longer be taken for granted. Hence, having a side hustle is important.

The arguments against it include:

- Employer's fear of conflict of interest.
- Employer's fear of breach of confidentiality.
- Inappropriate use of company resources (which can lead to security-related issues).
- Additionally, fatigue and burnout can occur from multiple engagements, which may lead to failure to deliver in their primary job.

The question is: Is this ethically and legally acceptable?

Now Indian law is not very clear in these areas, which then

become a subject of interpretation. In the absence of proper legal guidance, the job contract is the best document that can be referred to. Companies tend to enforce rules based on job contracts or offer letters.

If moonlighting or a side hustle does not conflict with the primary job, why is it a concern, or why should companies not allow their employees to do it?

I believe that moonlighting should be allowed if the employer's concerns are addressed. This will require two things from the employer:

- Proactively introduce a moonlighting policy. It may not be perfect, but it will evolve eventually.
- When a company embraces, acknowledges and accepts moonlighting, it creates an outcome-driven work culture so that an employee's productivity can be measured by what they deliver, not how much time they spend.

Swiggy has a moonlighting policy and allows its employees to moonlight provided the concerns are appropriately addressed.

At the time this book was written, Infosys had stringent policies in place, according to which a person found guilty of moonlighting was liable to face severe repercussions, including termination of employment.

As work from office begins with more vigour, more and more companies will have their own rules on moonlighting.

What I would love to see is if bigger companies will take

the lead and set employee-friendly policies or if they will just define the policy in terms of the usual 'penalty model'.

The New Workplace Model

When it seemed that people had fully accepted working from home, COVID showed signs of easing, and so the drive to bring people back to the office began. Employers now struggle to get their employees back into the office and are facing severe reluctance and attrition when trying to implement work from the office.

A CEO-friend of mine mentioned a very interesting challenge regarding his employees and working from the office drive. He said, 'Satyajit, when I ask my employees to come back to the office, they give me a plethora of reasons, like they are worried about the crowd, how to avoid infections, etc. But the same employee doesn't care when they go to a pub or disco or cinema or shopping mall. What should I do?'

Office Peacocking

The challenge the CEO spoke about is not his only one. Many leaders and organizations continue to face the daunting task of getting their employees back into the office. To entice employees back into the office, companies have resorted to what is known as 'office peacocking'. It is a trend where companies are making their offices more attractive to lure employees back. Common perks include renovating the space to make it more vibrant, colourful and aesthetic, games rooms, gourmet meals (sometimes free), etc. These initiatives are expected to encourage working from the office and bring more people back after prolonged remote working. However, the question is whether swanky initiatives such as 'office peacocking' can bring employees accustomed to working from home back to the office.

Well, opinion is divided. While a section of employees is happy to work from office, irrespective of office peacocking a large number still prefer to work from home. The majority, however, prefer a hybrid arrangement where you go into the office a certain number of times a month or week. So the challenge continues.

Perhaps many CEOs and leaders will opt for the Elon Musk way. Musk wrote emails to his employees urging them to come into the office or leave Tesla. He believed that companies that don't need their workforce at the office don't ship great products. Now these are just his views and outlook, but nothing is stopping other CEOs and leaders from taking a similar stand. Only time will tell what trend CEOs will embrace.

However, not all companies and leaders believe in the same theory. This has given rise to a third working model called the 'hybrid model'.

Put simply, the hybrid model refers to a working arrangement that requires employees to work in the office for a few days and the remaining from home.

Whilst both employers and employees are divided on the way forward, there must be a system where working from home and working in the office will coexist; we just don't know it yet.

That brings us to the question of what the expectations of work will be in the new age given the changing environment.

In my opinion, the majority of companies will opt for mixed options, and this mixed-options model could last a long time. There will be some companies that may start with a hybrid work week but slowly and surely force employees to return and not change their ways. Some companies are in the middle of this transition of making employees work all week in the office, and some have embraced work from office fully, often penalizing employees (through pay cuts, layoffs, etc.) who do not fall in line.

Nevertheless, there will be many companies that would like to make the hybrid working model a reality. For them, the biggest challenge would be measuring productivity and effectiveness. When working from home during COVID, coordination was a manager's nightmare as employees left their base location to work from the comfort of their homes. To create a successful hybrid model, the measurement of jobs needs to be outcome-driven and not the number of hours.

Surprisingly, measuring the outcome rather than the number of hours is not something that has not been tried successfully before. In 2004, Netflix, one of the most innovative new-age companies, started what is called the 'no vacation' policy. As draconian as it may sound, in reality it was far from it. The core idea was not to have a predetermined list of holidays that was mandatory for everyone but to give people the opportunity to take their vacations.

By doing so, Netflix put the power in the hands of its employees. The simple idea was to measure productivity not by the number of hours but in terms of targets (outcomes) achieved. I am not saying this is the perfect way, because every system has its challenges and limitations. But at least it is a bold attempt to make a paradigm shift to an outcome-based measurement model.

Companies that make this transition will require a mature workforce that can deliver results and not have to be pushed around, micromanaged and monitored by the hour. Unfortunately, the majority of the workforce lacks the drive and doesn't understand the nuances of an outcome-driven mindset. It remains to be seen how companies will evolve to meet this challenge.

Coffee Badging

As the hybrid model grew in popularity, many companies adopted the model where employees were expected to 'show up' a certain number of days a month or week. Perhaps employees took this 'showing up' literally and started coffee badging, a concept where employees show up at the office based on a roster. They just show up, spend a small amount of time, quickly touch base, and then head back home. This is real. A survey by Owl Labs called State of Hybrid Work 2023 found that 58 per cent of the respondents admitted to coffee badging. The question is, why are employees coffee badging? I happened to be talking to a co-worker about this, and he said: 'Look, there is no point travelling more than an hour to the office to do the same work that I can do from home. I come to the office because it is the company's mandate to show up. So I come and go at a time when I feel there is less traffic.' That could well be one of the reasons. How can one address this? One way is to have a clear agenda in mind in terms of planning your workday. Set clear goals regarding why you are coming to the office—for example, is this an opportunity to meet and network with leaders and co-workers? Focus on productivity rather than the number of hours in the office. Ultimately, I would say that coffee badging has the potential to dilute your strong work ethic. So be watchful.

Dry Promotion

In recent times, dry promotion has gained popularity among companies. Dry promotion is when an employee is promoted and receives a higher designation, but with no associated salary hike. While such moves provide employees with the promotions they are seeking, they leave them high and dry without the financial rewards generally associated with a promotion. Companies face pressure on their profit margins and also need to retain their employees. This is midway. Many people I know left companies immediately after their dry promotions. They waited to get the promotion title on their resumes. For example, an associate vice president of a company was promoted to a vice president's role. His resume immediately looked better, and he chose to leave the company. Dry promotion is here to stay, so it is better to come to terms with it as a working professional.

Work-Life Balance

This is one of the most common complaints. People tend to think that they don't have a work-life balance in their jobs. While this may be true, most people don't understand what work-life balance means.

Our outlook on our careers is mostly bookish. We tend to look at the happy path. We think we will take a job, work hard, get promoted, climb the career ladder, spend quality time with family and friends, and then be happy forever. But that's not the reality.

In reality, we need to understand work-life balance as a concept. Work-life balance doesn't mean that you work 50 per cent and live your life 50 per cent. Nor does it mean that you work for fixed hours and spend the rest of the time on your leisure activities, friends and family. The truth is that you have to imagine work and life together in the same bottle with a two-coloured liquid. Let's say work is red and life is green. Based on the phase of life, career choice and priorities, there will sometimes be more red than green and sometimes more green than red.

Juggling between red and green amidst changing priorities

is what work–life balance is all about. There will be times when you want to focus more on your career. At these times, you will have more red in the bottle than green. If you have more red by choice, then be willing to live with less green, and if you long for green at the same time, then you will always be stressed. Hence it is about setting the priorities right at different stages of life. Some significantly matured organizations offer their employees a dial-down model. If an employee opts for the dial-down model, they have to work half a day at half pay. Naturally, for them career progression will slow down. So what you have here is more green than red, as it is the same bottle.

Whether you want more green or more red at any given time depends entirely on your aspirations, phase of life, and life priorities. Once you know what you want more, be ready to accept the consequences and live with them.

Age-o-meter: Usefulness with Respect to Age

Some time ago, I came across a post on social media about how Queen Elizabeth held the crown until her death at the age of 96. The post contrasted this with how corporates view the usefulness and effectiveness of their employees in terms of age. A 40-year-old professional today feels threatened by the skills of a 30-year-old who could take over their position. Similarly, a 50-year-old is on his toes because he never knows when a 40-year-old may take his place in the organization. It seems that age is a measure of effectiveness, and the older you get, the less you stand a chance.

However, I take a slightly different view. If age were the only factor, then companies would have employees only up to a certain age. There would be no older employees in organizations. But this is not true. Every organization has a mix of old and new, experienced and new energy. Many organizations provide the opportunity to rejoin the company as a consultant after reaching retirement age. However, this trend about age and relevance is sadly true. But the reason is not just age. *It is and always has been about how relevant you are to the company's plan and your career.* No company puts the axe randomly on those who are over a certain age bracket. In a private enterprise, it is always about what you bring to the table.

A private job offers ample opportunities at every stage of the career. But as professionals, we also need to be aware of how each stage of our professional career unfolds, what opportunities are available, and what the expectations are. Once we understand these aspects, we need to find a way to stay competitive. As long as we are competitive and change our game as per expectations (at different levels), I don't see why companies should use an age-o-meter to determine our usefulness. But if a company does, thank your stars for not working in a regressive culture. Otherwise, every single day that you would have spent in the company would have been spent in fear—the fear of facing the axe any day.

There is a significant change in the workplaces operating today. Newer trends are emerging, and job tenure is becoming shorter and more volatile. In such an ever-changing environment, how should we look at our careers?

1. If you happen to be someone who has gained insight into work–life balance during the pandemic, do not let it go to waste. Opportunities to look at things differently don't come along every day. Embrace a version of work–life that works for you, and you will see how you can lead an engaging and fulfilling job life.
2. No matter what the situation is, an employee should not 'quiet quit'. If you are mentally checked out, even being the 'minimum guy' doesn't work. Do not compromise on your work ethic. Companies and jobs will come and go, but your work ethic will stay with you. Don't allow temporary winds to uproot it.
3. One of the biggest expectations employees must have of themselves is to understand how outcome-driven profiles work and what they can do to excel in them. Outcome-driven profiles are adopted by mature organizations where each role has a set of deliverables, a timeline and a defined process. Teams spend time and effort creating this clarity for each member, and each member then works on their track with suitable, well-defined, scheduled collaboration. This way of working requires you to be extremely efficient, well-organized and well-planned.
4. People who work or are working in a rather chaotic or ambiguous environment will not find it easy to adapt, and vice versa. Chaotic and ambiguous companies will always find it difficult to implement working from

home, hybrid models, etc. For them, the ultimate plan is to be back at the office. So be aware when choosing your next employer.

5. Eliminate the idea that age is a bar or a barrier. At any stage of your career, it's about understanding what's expected of you, reinventing yourself, and staying competitive and relevant to your career.

9

Freedom

'Freeing yourself was one thing, claiming ownership of that freed self was another.'

—Toni Morrison

Freedom—a very powerful concept in our lives. Many books and articles discuss this concept. Many associate freedom with financial independence and early retirement. A simple concept of having earned 'enough' money so that you no longer have to do something you might not like in order to earn money, but use your time to do something you do like.

It is like getting up in the morning and deciding for yourself what you want to do rather than having a prescribed list of things to do. Of course, I mentioned 'enough', and that's why freedom is personal, as each of us has a different number for that 'enough'. But what is the true meaning of freedom—is it just having enough money? If it means getting up in the morning and doing what you want to do, does that mean that working professionals cannot achieve freedom? Do you believe that entrepreneurs are free? They are not. They too must listen to others (their investors), even if they are executing their dream idea. *Freedom is not so much about what you do. It's more about how you do it.*

In this chapter, we will try to understand the concept of freedom and see if we can create a meaningful framework for ourselves: a framework that can be used by anyone, whether they work in a job or are an entrepreneur or anyone else.

To understand and define the kind of freedom I am talking about, we first need to understand a few underlying concepts.

Let us first understand the concept of money and earning and their role in freedom. Money is very important. After all, all worldly transactions are conducted through money. But can an excess of money give you freedom? The answer is no. Many people earn a lot of money and do not like the field they work in at all. This can happen in any field. Take the example of acting. Do you think that all stars have complete freedom because they have money? No. Many of them have to do things they feel forced to do because they are strategic to their work. Take the example of high-paying jobs. I know some of the very well-paid professionals in the Indian market, and when I see them, they are not free either. They have to do certain things against their will. So having money is one of the factors of freedom, but it is not 'the factor'.

Let's examine another dimension. Nowadays, the concept of FIRE (Financial Independence, Retire Early) is a hot topic. This means investing early on and earning enough by a certain age to be able to quit your job and do things you like. The whole premise is based on the hypothesis that people don't like to work and can only pursue their goals if they can retire early. My first book, *Work, Workmanship and Winning,* was the exact opposite of this and was based on the idea that corporate jobs can also be engaging and fulfilling. If that's the case, why do you need to retire early?

Let's say you have enough money and could quit doing what you are doing (because you don't like it and are only doing it for the money); what would you do with the time you have freed up? Would you just sit around? Have you planned something worthwhile to keep yourself meaningfully engaged?

A very senior professional worked in some of the top companies in India. He held senior leadership roles, and his current C-level position has a compensation of over 1.5 crores. However, he is struggling in his current job because he doesn't like the work, as there is too much micro-management, etc. Do you think he doesn't have enough money to retire early? He has much more than what the retirement calculators can project for him. Yet he is battling it out in the corporate world. Why is that? I was very curious and asked him why he wanted to keep going when he could hang up his boots. He replied quite simply, 'Satyajit, I just don't know what to do if I don't have this kind of work. I might not like it in the current company, but this is what I do.' Freedom is not just about having money. It also has to do with what can keep us meaningfully engaged.

People who think that once they have money they don't need to do anything will never understand the true meaning of freedom. Having financial independence is not freedom.

You have to understand what you want to do with your free time. How can you be meaningfully engaged with things that you derive satisfaction from? In case you realize what you have chosen to do is not what you want to do, look for the next gig.

So far we have discussed money and having something that can occupy us meaningfully. Is that all, or is there more to it than that?

We all enjoy some kind of appreciation for what we do. Even when we dare to do things we want to do ourselves. When I wrote my first book, a reader who bought my book connected with me on LinkedIn and mentioned how much he liked my book and my ideas. He said he was eagerly awaiting my next book. After this recognition, I was instantly on cloud nine. After all, it's one thing to appreciate the book, but here's a reader looking forward to the next book. I was elated.

We do a lot of things. Some create content, some write, some make movies, and some do something else (other than jobs). In many cases, people also make money this way. But the question is: even if you are engaged and earn money, is that enough to give you a sense of freedom? No. You need some kind of recognition. Not necessarily from the public. It could be your recognition—about a book written to your satisfaction, a YouTube video where you were able to share the information appropriately, or a post on social media enabling you to express yourself (that may not even go viral). One must have a certain amount of self-knowledge, a certain amount of well-being, and, God willing, a certain amount of recognition from the target audience. Even if we go into a job, do you think you're really happy there if you're earning well and are committed but don't get any recognition? In this sense, recognition is crucial.

The fourth element I would like to discuss with regard to freedom is evolution. We must evolve in whatever we do. The repetition of activities turns us into machines, not individuals.

A recruiter posted a story on LinkedIn about a young man she was trying to hire for a new opportunity. The new opportunity was a big step-up from his current position. However, he declined the offer, stating that he was not interested. Naturally curious, the recruiter wanted to find out the reason. The candidate replied that he had already made it to the top. This answer baffled the recruiter, as he was far from being at the top. He was a long way down the hierarchy. Obviously, he was explaining that getting to the top meant for him that he loved the work he did every day, that he loved the company that treated him well, that he had a good work–life balance, etc. This for him was making it to the top.

Although what he said is true, I believe that you cannot do the same thing over and over again. He can't keep on doing the same thing over and over again in the same company. It is not good either for him or the company. If he continues like this, the time will come when the same company that treats him well today will not think twice about showing him the door. The most important point is that this may be his reality today, but he needs to constantly evolve and change himself; otherwise it will not make the same sense to him later.

This is also true for entrepreneurs and solopreneurs.

In my mentorship programme, I mentor mid-level and senior professionals. It has a structure and a form aligned with the needs of professionals and is in tune with current developments. However, if I offer the same thing forever, it won't work, as the world is changing, and if my programme doesn't evolve further, it becomes repetitive for me and obsolete for my clients and ultimately creates value for none. Hence evolution is very critical.

Let me now present you with a synthesis of all that I have discussed as a key takeaway. I call it the 4E framework for freedom. The 4Es stand for: **e**arning, **e**ngagement, **e**minence and **e**volution.

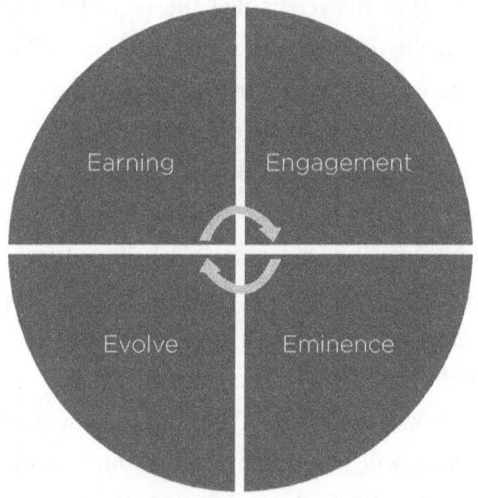

Let me quickly describe it to you. As I mentioned earlier, it's not so much about what you do but more about how you do it.

Earning

Simply put, it's about what you do for a living. Some people earn a living with a job, others through a profession (e.g., doctors, actors, etc.), some are entrepreneurs, and some may even be solopreneurs. It's different if you have rental incomes or investments that are self-sustaining in nature, which means they are mostly on autopilot. It doesn't matter. As long as you earn X and your expenses are Y and X-Y is positive, everything is fine.

Many of us believe that money gives freedom. Yes, it gives us freedom in terms of the choices that money can buy. But that's about it. Nevertheless, there is no freedom without money.

Engagement

Imagine a scenario where you earn a lot of money. However, you are not meaningfully engaged. Let me elaborate on this further. A friend of mine had a profile in the growth and strategy function. Much of his career was spent in conglomerates, working on revenue programmes, new market entries, new product strategies, etc. Most of his roles were based in the CEO or the business head's office, and he has worked predominantly in head offices. For some personal reasons, he took a job that did not align with his skills. The pay was good and offered a lot of flexibility, but the role offered no learning or growth opportunities. He kept the job only to feel dragged to work. This experience did two things. First, he lost touch with what he was doing, and second, he had a sense of fear about what would happen if someone found out that he had mentally checked out. Will he be laid off?

Engaging meaningfully is very important because it makes you feel alive. What do I mean by 'being meaningfully engaged'? Being meaningfully engaged means feeling connected to what you do. Whatever work you do, you should feel motivated and excited about it. This may not always be possible but at least try to find something about your work that excites you. If you don't, trust me, you will not only be disconnected but also run the risk of becoming obsolete.

Eminence

We all crave a little attention here and there. But if you base your system of recognition on externalities, you are bound to be disappointed. When I first started writing on LinkedIn, like many other content creators, I wrote, posted and looked for likes and comments. When posts get likes and comments, I feel elated, and when they don't, I am disappointed. But I quickly realized that this model of eminence, where you depend on external recognition, is doomed to fail. So what is the solution? In my case, I no longer wrote for likes and comments as the end goal, but for 'self-expression'. The minute I changed this end goal, I was not chasing likes and comments but I was looking at each post as a means to express my ideas, and trust me, I have never been disappointed after that for my posts. It doesn't matter how many people liked it or shared it. Nor am I bothered about the famed and ever-changing algorithms of social media. I just write freely to express myself.

Evolution

This is a supercritical aspect of the framework. Nobody likes doing the same thing over and over again all their life. So we must evolve. We must evolve what we deliver, and we must work towards evolving with the right awareness.

The question is, how do we achieve these 4Es? Will I find something that offers all of these? The 4Es can come from one source (job, profession, etc.) or from multiple sources. Earning and engagement can come from the job; eminence and evolution can come from the hobby or passion or profession, etc. The idea is to achieve the 4Es in a way that creates a sense of freedom.

The next important point is how much of each E is needed. The answer to this question is the famous phrase 'it depends'. Every human being is different and their needs in relation to each E are also different. It is up to an individual to find the balance of the 4Es. It's just like the work–life balance at work. Everyone has their sweet spot.

There is still a critical aspect of freedom that I want to take up. Have you ever found yourself in a situation where you made an unconventional decision and then felt the urge to explain to others why you made that decision? Or have you ever been in a situation where you made a decision that you didn't want to follow through and wanted to take a U-turn but were just too worried about what people would think? This happens to many of us. True freedom is when you can break these shackles, when you do not feel the need to justify your choices to others.

To be able to do this, we must shift the focus from 'they' to 'I'.

Our mindset is such that we always give more importance to the likes, dislikes and opinions of others about ourselves. For example, when I drop my child off to classes during office hours and come back home, will people think I don't have a job, or worse, that I was fired? We seem to put what THEY think above what is important to us. The greatest freedom is not worrying about what others think or feeling the urge to explain it to them. It is about understanding what is important to you and being sure of it.

Freedom is mostly associated and understood with financial freedom, but as you have observed, many other dimensions together complete the sense of freedom.

- Freedom means not being bound by rules and regulations but also not being disrespectful.
- Freedom is not what you can do but what you choose to do.
- Freedom is not just getting up in the morning and deciding what you want to do.
- Freedom is completing the 4Es of your life.
- Freedom is your conviction about your choices and overcoming the urge to explain or feel apologetic about your choices to others.

10

The Right Lens

We all look at the world through our lenses, shaped by our experiences, beliefs and emotions. But what if we are looking through the wrong one? What if our lens is clouded by past conditioning, fears or limited thinking? The right lens isn't about ignoring difficulties or blind optimism. Rather, it's about developing a mindset that embraces both challenges and possibilities, allowing us to see the bigger picture while actively shaping our path. It helps us prioritize what truly matters, let go of what we can't control, and channel our energy into areas where we can make a difference. While the right lens is deeply personal, it is also based on the nine themes underpinning the universal tenets—self-awareness, resilience and growth.

Getting the Right Lens

You don't just wake up one day and find it in place. You earn it. The right lens emerges when you undergo a personal transformation. But change is not a one-off event; it's an ongoing process. Every setback, every challenge, and every moment of self-doubt is an opportunity to reinvent yourself, shift your perspective and emerge stronger.

What then should be the outcome of a personal transformation? This is a very profound question that requires some thought. Is the result of the transformation something big that the world can recognize? Or is the transformation something deeper, more personal and independent of external validation?

Not every transformation leads to a visible or measurable result—and it doesn't have to. The outcome of personal transformation isn't the destination, but the journey itself. It is the process itself that changes you from the inside out and changes the way you look at life.

Framework for Transformation

The nine life themes will hopefully enable you to embark on your personal transformation journey as they aim to change you from within. The nine themes provide a framework for understanding our inner self from a different perspective. Each of the nine themes connects you to an important aspect of life and our interactions with it:

- How do we define success?
- How do we handle setbacks?
- What truly shapes our identity?
- How do we make decisions in everyday life?

- How do hobbies enrich our lives in ways we often ignore?
- Why is it important to reach out and ask for help, and why is it so hard?
- Why is giving back to society important, and how can it fulfil us?
- What is our relationship to our career?
- What does true freedom mean?

These themes are an attempt to give my readers a new perspective—their version of the right lens with which they can craft their unique journey.

The perspective you develop from these nine themes is not static. As time passes and circumstances change, your understanding and reflection on these nine themes must change. That's the true hallmark of personal transformation—not just adopting a new perspective but allowing it to evolve over time.

The True Trigger of Transformation

When we think about the idea of transformation, a fundamental question remains: How does it begin? What triggers it?

For a long time, I believed that transformation is triggered by circumstances—that we only change when life forces us to. Then I asked myself, 'What if certain events never happen? Does that mean there will never be a transformation?'

I kept searching for an answer. I kept asking myself, 'How will I find the trigger? Who is going to give the trigger?'

One evening, as I sat in my living room pondering these questions, my eyes drifted toward a large mirror across the room. I saw my reflection. I looked at myself, really looked at myself. And in that moment, I understood something powerful: We don't have to wait for external circumstances to push us toward change. Transformation can begin in a quiet moment, a fleeting realization, or a simple glance in the mirror. It happens the moment we decide to see the world through a new lens—not the one handed to us, but the one we choose to create.

I looked at my reflection again. In the silence, it was as if this reflection whispered back, 'Just get on with it.'

Acknowledgements

Writing a book is a bit like painting: you bring your imagination to life. In the course of writing, there will be occasional moments when a brushstroke here and there threatens to ruin the painting or could well be a masterstroke. Often, in those moments of pain, my editors Yamini Chowdhury, Richa Tewari and Sana Yaseen stood by my side lending a sense of direction and guidance. I am extremely thankful to them. Special note of thanks to Aurodeep Mukherjee for being one of the first readers.

I am grateful to my publisher for choosing my manuscript from the hundreds they receive daily. Thank you for the vote of confidence. It has certainly encouraged me to stay the course.

I would like to thank my father Shri Rabinarayan Senapati, who read the manuscript for accuracy and flow, and my wife Smaranika for being a generous critic. My daughter Sanskriti played a significant role in the book. She encouraged me, clapped for me and gave me a high five every time I completed a chapter. I would also like to acknowledge my sister Sonali for her unwavering support.

I am very thankful to my readers who have read my previous works and always shared their honest feedback. It has pushed me to do better as an author.

www.ingramcontent.com/pod-product-compliance
Lightning Source LLC
Chambersburg PA
CBHW021158160426
43194CB00007B/790